Save Me a Spot In Heaven

Save Me a Spot In Heaven

Copyright © 2013 by Bailey Wind with Chris Graf

Cover design by Christi DiNinni

Book design by Cory Freeman

Printed in the United States of America

The Troy Book Makers
Troy, New York • thetroybookmakers.com

To order additional copies of this title, contact
www.spotinheaven.com

ISBN: 978-1-61468-191-5

Save Me a Spot
In Heaven

A Loving Tribute
to Christopher F. Stewart #69

Bailey Wind

with Chris Graf

I dedicate this book to my boyfriend and best friend Christopher F. Stewart, his parents Mike and Regina Stewart, and his brother Jeremy Stewart. They are and always will be my family. I love them very much!

Acknowledgement

I believe that certain people are put in your life for a reason. I know Chris was.

A chance meeting of a Shenendehowa mom at the TGIF's in Clifton Park, New York after attending Christmas Eve mass with Chris's parents made this book a reality.

Chris Graf, a freelance writer, unexpectedly ran into my family that night and kindly gave us a gift card to pay for our meal. She recognized me from the news and has a daughter who was a classmate of Chris and Deanna's. It didn't end there. Ms. Graf reached out to me later and said that if I ever wanted to write anything she would love to help me. She didn't expect me to say yes, but I did. I told her that I wanted to write a book about Chris.

It is because of her compassion, time, good heart, and belief in my story that this book was created. I am forever grateful to her.

I would also like to thank Mrs. Eileen Riley-Hall, an English teacher at Shenendehowa High School, for volunteering her time to edit this book. And thank you to Christi DiNinni of Roma Designs for volunteering to design my book cover.

And finally, I would like to thank my mom. She has always been my greatest supporter, and she is always by my side. She encourages me to do my best and to follow my dreams. She is my role model. She is an amazing mom to me and Nikki, and she is a cancer survivor. My mom manages to remain positive and strong, and she never lets me give up on myself. I would be nowhere without her, and she helped make this book a reality.

Moving away from home to attend college will be hard because I have always been a homebody. But I know that my mom will come running the second that I say that I need her. She is the one who will give me strength to pursue my diving career. A lot of people say that they have the best mom in the world, but I really do.

Mom, you are my best friend. I hope that someday I can be as good of a mother as you are. I love you!

A Message from Dawn Wind

Bailey Wind is my daughter, and I encouraged her to write this book for many reasons. The main reason is simple: Bailey and Chris's story is amazing from start to finish. When you learn where Chris lived you will understand why I believe they were meant to meet. It was fate. Their love wasn't a typical teenage puppy love. They stayed committed to each other even when others tried to come between them. Their story reminds me of a Greek tragedy. Their tragic ending came on the night of December 1, 2012.

Bailey's book focuses on more than just her relationship with Chris. She also writes about bullying, self-image, forgiveness, social media, kindness, and grief. I hope that everyone who reads this book learns something from it. I hope that teenagers learn to think about the consequences of their actions, and I hope that parents realize how important it is to monitor what their children are doing online. Parents need to take action to end cyber-bullying.

Although this book is a tribute to Chris Stewart, I thought you would like to know a little bit about Bailey. After the accident, people saw pictures of her on the news. They learned she was an elite diver who was headed to the University of Tennessee. Many people formed a picture of her in their mind and assumed that she was a girl who was full of self-confidence. They were wrong.

Bailey has always had a hard time in the social and self-confidence areas. She attended a Catholic school from kindergarten through fourth grade. Each year she would make a best friend only to have that friend transfer to another school at the end of the year. This was especially difficult for Bailey because she was so quiet and shy. Losing so many friends had an impact on her, and I believe that it made her hesitant to reach out and form new friendships. In fifth grade, she transferred into the public school system where she knew no one. She was a tomboy and never felt like she fit in—while the other girls were wearing makeup, tight jeans, and low-cut shirts, Bailey was wearing basketball shorts, t-shirts, a ponytail, and no makeup. The kids were cruel to her: they excluded her, made fun of her, and bullied her. Despite their cruelty, Bailey stayed true to herself. She would not change for anyone, not even to fit in.

I believe sports saved Bailey. Bailey was active in swimming, diving, gymnastics, basketball, and Irish step dance for many years. We juggled it all until we felt she needed to put all her energy into one sport. To my delight, she chose diving. Diving gave her something to focus on; it made her feel good about herself. She started diving for her Varsity high school team as a seventh grader. She also dove for a travel team and trained at RPI in Troy, New York. She dove for both teams until eleventh grade. She would leave one practice and eat dinner in the car on the way to the next practice. Since the age of nine, Bailey has worked tirelessly to achieve her goal of diving for a Division One college team. Training and school work have been her life.

In 10th grade, Bailey underwent a total physical transformation. She was styling. She had long legs like a model, a thin figure, and a beautiful Hollywood smile from years of orthodontics. She was a stand-out on the Varsity diving team, traveled all over for competitions with her travel dive team, and started to come out of her shell. But the bullying didn't end. Bailey could never understand why it was happening and either could we. It was painful, and I admire her for the way she handled it. Although she was called names and sent nasty Facebook messages from kids she didn't know, she took the high road and never responded to any of it.

Eleventh grade was a real breakthrough year for Bailey. She made the difficult decision to dive for just one team—her travel team. This allowed her to focus more on her studies. During this time, she was friended by a group of girls she had known since elementary school. Finally, after all those terrible lonely years, the bullying seemed to be over. Bailey had friends to hang out with. It was during that same year that she caught the eye of Christopher F. Stewart. Her years of feeling so alone were over. Her Prince Charming had come knocking!

I think it's fair to say every mother of a teenage girl has certain fears when their daughter starts to date. I know I did. But I couldn't have picked a better boyfriend for

Bailey than Chris Stewart. His parents did an amazing job raising him. I texted his mom several times during their relationship and told her those exact words. I felt blessed that he was Bailey's boyfriend. Chris was every mother's dream boyfriend for their teenage daughter. I felt God had rewarded Bailey for all the pain she suffered at the hands of others by giving her Chris. I even wished they had met later in life because he was "The One", and I dreaded the day they would go off to different colleges. I knew that it would be very difficult for both of them.

Over the years, I stood by my daughter and watched as she progressed from being silent to having a voice for herself. I think the love Chris showed Bailey helped her find her voice. Bailey was finally able to stand up for herself, and she did. Unfortunately, there are those that can never win no matter how they respond to nastiness. I believe that to be true for Bailey.

To say I am proud of Bailey would be an understatement. Bailey has always been so strong-willed and determined. Several years ago, she set her sights on the University of Tennessee; she looked at other colleges but only applied to Tennessee. She knew what she wanted, and she made it happen. Bailey overcame a lot of insecurities and rejection from her peers, and she has worked extremely hard at her academics. Her strength continues to amaze me. I witness it on a daily basis as she deals with pain and struggles that are invisible to the rest of the world. In addition to dealing with the pain of losing Chris and Deanna, she continues to deal with the bullying and criticism that she received AFTER the accident.

In her low moments and at times when her insecurities surface, I remind her of something so very valuable. There was this special kid named Chris Stewart. He was loved by all who knew him. And he chose her, Bailey Wind, as the girl that he loved. She was his one and only, now and forever.

Bailey will move forward. I know she will. I also know she will carry the pain of losing Chris with her for the rest of her life. But Chris will always be with her. He will keep her strong and guide her way. I believe in my heart that somehow, in some way, Chris saved Bailey's life on the night of the accident. He did, I just know he did. Chris loved her that much.

Preface

I am only seventeen years old, but I have learned what it is like to have lived, loved, and lost. I survived a horrific car accident that killed my boyfriend, Christopher Stewart, and my dear friend Deanna Rivers. I suffered terrible physical injuries during the accident, but it is my emotional scars that will be the most difficult to heal. I will carry them with me for the rest of my life.

Even though Chris and I were only seventeen, we shared a special kind of love that some people never get to experience during an entire lifetime. Ours was a love story between two teenagers from different high schools. We had many things in common including a strong commitment to athletics. Chris was one of the captains of his high school football team, and I was a competitive springboard diver on a travel diving team. Chris played football from the time that he was a young boy, and I started taking diving lessons when I was nine years old.

When we started dating, I was a junior at Shaker High School in Latham, New York, and Chris was a junior at Shenendehowa (Shen) High School in Clifton Park, New York. We never imagined that being from different high schools would be a problem. But it was a problem—a big problem. Many of Chris's friends never accepted our relationship, and this left Chris feeling very torn. He was not a person who enjoyed confrontation. He was a big teddy bear; some people called him Stewz. He just wanted everyone to be happy. Chris loved me, and he loved his friends as well. He had room for all of us in his life, but sadly, some of his friends had no room for me in theirs.

The problems that we encountered tested our relationship and proved how strong our love for one another was. We felt as if it was strong enough to survive anything, but we were wrong. Chris did not survive the accident on the night of December 1, 2012. I did. My memories, pictures, and messages are all that I have left of him.

My life will never be the same without Chris in it. I have cried more tears in the past months than I have cried in my entire life. My heart aches so badly I can't even describe the feeling. I feel lost and alone even though I have so much support from a loving family, friends, and the entire community.

My grief takes many forms. I grieve alone in my room. I grieve during my therapy appointments. I grieve on social media. I grieve with my friends. I grieve with my family. I grieve with Chris's family. And through this book, I grieve with you.

As I grieve, my body continues to heal from my many physical injuries. My days are frequently filled with doctor and dentist appointments. I attend benefits in honor of the car accident victims and their families; I try to attend them all to show how thankful I am for everyone's support. I attended many of these events while wearing a neck brace and displaying a row of missing front teeth. I would have preferred not to be seen by the world that way, but I did it to honor Chris.

During this time, I have been faced with some unexpected challenges. I have been bullied, judged, and told how I should be grieving. Some of this has taken place on social media, and some has taken place in person. It is still hard for me to believe that this has happened.

I am recovering from my physical injuries, but I continue to feel shattered on the inside. People who see me in public or in television interviews are amazed by how good I look. They don't see me during my darkest moments that take place in the security of my home. During many of these moments, I have comforted myself by writing this book. This is my tribute to Chris and my way of celebrating his life and preserving our memories. I don't ever want to stop feeling his strength, kindness, energy, personality, happiness, and love. I felt all of those things on December 1, 2012, the last time we were together. I still feel them today. I will carry Chris with me forever.

In Memory of Christopher F. Stewart
January 9, 1995 – December 1, 2012

CHAPTER 1

||||||||||||||||||||||||||||||||||||||||||||||||||||||||||||||||||||||||||||||||||||||||||||||||||||||||||||||||||||||||||||||||||||||||||||

December 1, 2012

I woke up on Saturday, December 1, 2012 expecting it to be a great day. My family had tickets to the Siena College vs. University of Albany basketball game, and I looked forward to this game every year. My sister, Nikki, and I have been going to Siena basketball games with our parents for as long as I can remember. It is just something fun that we do together.

My boyfriend, Chris, was going to the game with us, and I had also invited our friends Deanna and Matt. Deanna hadn't thought that she would be able to go, so I was really excited when she texted me that morning and said they were coming.

Chris played football for Shenendehowa High School, and he had a football banquet at Shaker High School that morning. I didn't go with him, but my friend who was there texted me and told me how nice Chris looked all dressed up with his hair all slicked back. That made me smile.

Chris came over after the banquet, and we went for a walk with my dad and our dog, Moose. We also spent time talking to my mom about different things and what Chris and I did the night before. My mom showed us some University of Tennessee clothing she had purchased for my grandfather for Christmas. Chris asked my mom what she wanted for Christmas. He said he wanted to get her something nice because she was so good to him. My mom told him not to waste his money on her; she said she just wanted him to keep her daughter happy. We also watched Dinner for Shmucks. We loved to watch movies together—especially scary ones. We would always end up talking, laughing, and goofing around so much that sometimes we would miss most of the movie. Chris and I loved to laugh and could talk about anything and everything together. There was never a dull moment when he was around.

Deanna and Matt came over to my house to hang out before we left for the game that night. I was so happy to see Deanna because we didn't get to spend much time together during the school year because we went to different schools. Deanna was a good friend of Chris's from Shen, and I met her when I went to Shen's junior prom in May 2012. She was so nice to me right from the start, and we became fast friends. She was someone I could always trust, and I could tell her anything. Her boyfriend, Matt, was a year younger than Chris and the two were on the football team together. The four of us had so much fun hanging out together. Before we left for the game Deanna spent some time showing my mom her senior pictures. She looked so beautiful.

My parents were going to the game with us, and we all piled into one car. I'm a hard-core Siena fan, so I was really into the game. Chris, on the other hand, wasn't very interested in basketball and decided that he would cheer for UAlbany. His reason? Because UAlbany's uniforms are purple and purple was his favorite color! Every time there was a break in the action, Chris and my mom would high-five each other and sing in my ears to try to get me going. I let them have their fun and pretended to be annoyed, but I actually thought it was pretty funny.

At one point during the game, long balloons were being thrown into the crowd from the balcony. A yellow one landed near us, and I grabbed it and wrapped it around Chris's head. He wore it proudly, and my mom snapped a few pictures. Chris had no problem mugging for the camera. I still have that balloon. It's stretched out and deflated, but it makes me smile when I think of Chris wearing it on his head. At one point Deanna said she wanted a balloon too. Chris told her to let the little kids have the balloons. Meanwhile, he was sitting there with his yellow balloon on his head. We all just laughed.

Siena lost that night, but the night was so much fun that it didn't matter to me. Chris laid in the back of my mom's car on the way home and took a nap. He nearly rolled out when we got home and opened the back hatch. Chris always had a way of making me laugh even when he wasn't trying.

The four of us went into my house and watched the last twenty minutes of Elf. That was Deanna's favorite movie, and it always made her laugh. Deanna invited me to sleep over at her house, and we asked my sister Nikki to come too. Nikki packed her overnight bag but changed her mind at the last minute and decided not to go. I will always be grateful for that last-minute decision.

We said goodbye to my family and got into Chris's

Explorer. The four of us were going to hang out at Deanna's house; her parents had pizza waiting for us. I don't remember much after that, but I do remember Chris's SUV being hit very hard from behind. The car that hit us seemed to come out of nowhere; it happened so quickly there was nothing Chris could have done to avoid the accident. I remember hearing Chris yell, and then things went black.

I can piece together what happened next although it is very surreal when I think about it. After the car hit us, the SUV rolled over, and I must have blacked out. When I opened my eyes, the vehicle was on its side. I was on the side of the vehicle that had landed on the ground, and all of the windows were smashed. My shoes were off, and my feet were freezing. I remember feeling confused and thinking that I was in a dream. When I heard Matt's voice, I realized that I wasn't dreaming. I never heard Chris or Deanna. I don't remember what Matt said, but it sounded like he was outside of the vehicle. I started yelling and screaming and pushing against something with my feet in a desperate and frantic attempt to get out of the Explorer. I felt cramped in a very small space, and it was terrifying.

I don't remember the rescue crew arriving, but I was aware that there were bright lights shining on me. I was so scared, and I kept telling myself I was dreaming. The paramedics were repeatedly asking me my name and telling me not to move. I don't remember them pulling me out of the wreck, but I do remember them putting a blanket over my face. They used the blanket to protect my face while they were using the Jaws of Life to get me out of the wreckage. I'm grateful that I can only remember the blanket. Despite my injuries, I don't remember being in any physical pain because my body was in shock.

As all of this was happening, I had no idea of what was unfolding at my house. Matt's mom had been on her way home and passed a horrible accident—our accident —on the Northway (I 87N) and immediately became worried. Since her attempts to contact Matt failed, she called my mom at about 10:45 PM to see if Matt was still at the house. My mom told her we were at Deanna's, but Matt's mom had already called Deanna's house and was told we weren't there yet. My mom told her she would get ahold of me and Chris and have us tell Matt to call her. It wasn't until my mom tried to send texts to me and to Chris that she began to get worried. Because we have iPhones, she could tell that her texts were not being received. She knew then that something was wrong with both our phones. She also knew at that moment that something terrible had happened.

At that point, my dad, mom, and sister jumped into the car and sped up the Northway. Traffic was backed up, so they had to drive on the side of the road to get to the accident site. As my dad drove, my mom called Chris's mom. She was desperately hoping that we had stopped at Chris's house. My mom then called 911 and asked if they knew the ages and/or who the victims were in the accident, but they did not. As soon as my family arrived at the scene, they saw big construction lights set up on the highway to illuminate the accident scene. They also saw ambulances, state troopers, fire trucks, and rescuers on ladders; they were up in the trees holding additional lights. And then they saw it—the SUV. It had gone off the highway and was lying on its side in the trees. They recognized the vehicle immediately as being Chris's. Nikki screamed, "It's Chris's truck." When my mom saw how mangled it was, she turned away from it in horror. She didn't think there was any way anyone could have survived such a terrible accident.

Nikki was hysterical and my mom tried to calm her down. My mom was unbelievably calm and later said that she felt like she was having an out of body experience. She was in shock. My dad wasn't thinking clearly and started to drive away from the accident after a state trooper told him that he couldn't stay there. My mom yelled out that their daughter was in the SUV. That was when the trooper asked them what my name was and told my family to stay on the side of the highway in their vehicle.

My mom called Chris's mom and Deanna's mom and told both of them "It's them and it's really, really bad." Deanna's dad was already on his way to the scene. My mom tried to get ahold of Chris's dad and left him a frantic message for him to call her immediately. He was on his way home and was stuck in the traffic jam behind the accident when he received messages from my mom and Chris's mom. He was able to drive up the side of the road to get to the accident site.

Matt was the first to be cut out of the wreckage. Nikki saw him in the ambulance, and my mom was able to quickly relay the information to Matt's mother that he was alive, talking, and on his way to Albany Medical Center.

It took almost two hours for the rescue crew to get me out of the car, and my family had no idea if I was alive. I can't even imagine what they must have been going through. While they waited, my dad pounded his fists on the steering wheel and yelled, "No, no!" My mom phoned my grandfather who was on vacation in Florida. She told him we were in a terrible accident and that she didn't know if I was alive. She instructed him to call all of her siblings.

My mom and Nikki made their way back to Chris's dad's car. Nikki was so upset that she began throwing up on the side of the highway. A short time later, my mom saw rescue workers bring someone else out of the wreck in a stretcher. It was me, but she didn't know it at the time. When the state police officer finally told my family I was alive, my mom broke down and cried hysterically.

My family rushed to meet me at the hospital and waited anxiously for news on my condition. Matt's mom was already with him at the hospital when my family arrived. They asked to see me and were told that only Matt was there. The ambulance had left the scene before my parents, so my mom could think of only one reason why I wasn't at the hospital. She feared I had not survived the ambulance ride. Much to the relief of my family, the hospital staff checked again and discovered I was there. As my parents were being led back to see me, the nurse told them there had been two fatalities at the accident scene. My mom immediately dropped to her knees. She sobbed and said Chris and Deanna's names out loud. My dad sat down in a nearby chair, head in his hands, and cried. Both my parents had to pull themselves together before they entered my ER room.

I can't even imagine how scared they were when they walked into my room. I was wearing a neck brace, and my mouth and face were covered with blood and cuts. My top four front teeth and one lower tooth had been knocked out, but it looked as if I had lost every tooth in my mouth. My mouth looked like it was full of blood. My lips were cut, swollen and covered in fresh and dried blood. My nose was filled with dried blood. I was so cold that I was shaking uncontrollably even though there were heat lamps positioned around me. I was cold to the touch, and my mouth looked crooked when I spoke.

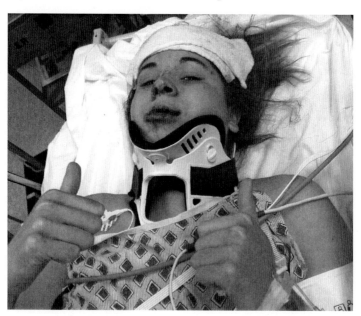

As soon as I saw my mom, the first thing I told her was that my grandma was with me. I told her I could smell my grandma's perfume. My mom was astonished and said, "Yes, Bailey. I know she is with you."

My grandma – my mom's mother – died four years ago after a courageous ten-month battle with cancer. During that ten month period, my grandma continually told me that she would always watch over me when she died. She kept that promise, and I know she was with me at the accident. I smelled her perfume while I was trapped in the SUV. I could still smell it when my parents got to the hospital. It really comforted me to know she was with me. My grandma died at the Albany Medical Center, the same hospital that I was taken to after the accident.

Nikki was afraid to come in to see me at first—she was afraid of how I would look—but I kept asking for her. She finally came in, and I was so happy to see my sister; we are very close. It felt good to have Nikki there holding my hand. She told me that I kept saying we had to hang out more and promised that we were going to hang out when I came home. My mom's sisters and brother came in to see me as well. I told my family how happy I was to see them because I didn't think I was ever going to see them again. I also told them how happy I was to be alive and asked if I was going to be okay.

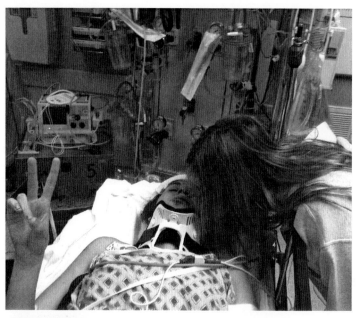

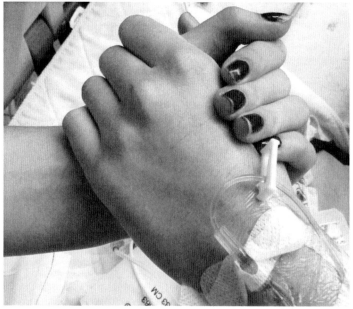

While all of this was happening, I was receiving a lot of painkillers to help with the pain from my broken neck, broken jaw, pulmonary contusions, swollen and bruised foot and leg, numerous abrasions, and knocked-out teeth. I didn't know my teeth had been knocked out, but I must have known something wasn't right because I told my mom I thought I needed a new retainer. My mom replied, "Umm, I think you need a little more than that honey."

Doctors were trying to assess my alertness and determine if I had any brain damage. I had some slight bleeding on the brain, so they kept asking me a lot of questions over and over. Apparently, I was reciting math formulas, singing the words to a song, and talking incessantly. The doctors were also worried about the possibility of paralysis. They informed my parents it was a good sign that I could move my legs, hands, and toes. I went through all kinds of tests, including CT scans and X-rays, so that they could identify all my injuries. When I found out my neck was broken, I panicked. Over and over, I asked every hospital staff member that entered my room if I was going to need surgery. I have always been scared to death of surgery.

I was in the emergency room for a long time before they moved me to the Pediatric Intensive Care Unit. A nurse came into my emergency room at one point and asked my mom to step out into the hall. I didn't know it, but Chris's dad had arrived at the hospital and asked to see my mom so that he could give her a hug. As my mom walked down the hallway, she saw Chris's dad slumped against the wall. It looked as if the wall was holding him up. As they hugged, she broke down and sobbed. The first thing Chris's dad said was, "I was hoping they'd be together forever." My own family had wished for the same thing.

I started asking for Chris almost right away. My parents felt it was best to wait until all my surgeries were over to tell me about Chris and Deanna, and the doctors and therapists agreed. They felt I needed all my strength to get through the surgeries. Every time I asked about Chris, they told me his parents were with him just like they were with me. I asked for him constantly over the course of the next several days. I asked if I could be brought to his room or if he could be brought to mine. I even asked if we could share the same hospital room. I would ask my mom to go to his room and tell him that I was thinking about him. Each day, I would ask if she had spoken to his parents. My parents finally told me he was at a different hospital; they thought it would put my mind at ease. I'm not mad at them for lying to me. I know how hard it must have been for them. They loved Chris too, but they knew I wasn't strong enough to hear the news. They were consulting with mental health professionals at the hospital, and everyone had my best interest in mind.

Doctors operated on my broken neck on Sunday, the day after the accident. I had four broken vertebrae, and one of them was totally smashed. The bone fragments from the smashed vertebrae were especially dangerous because they were close to my spinal canal and if moved any closer it could have caused me to become paralyzed. I'm very grateful to the doctors who operated on me and prevented this from happening. I will tell you though; I was not thrilled when my surgeon told me I had to have surgery. After he left my room, I told my mom she had to talk to him and tell him I needed to wait to have the surgery until Friday. I told her to please explain to him that I had high anxiety, that I was not ready, and that I needed more time. I told every hospital staff member (even the person cleaning my room) the same thing when they entered my room. I was told I was like a broken record; a heavily medicated broken record. Of course, I had no choice. It had to be done, but that didn't stop me from trying to put it off.

When I was wheeled into the operating area, I heard them say that operating room number 13 was ready. I said to my mom, "That's not for me is it? That number is unlucky; I don't want that room please."

On Monday, the day after my neck surgery, doctors operated on me once again. This time it was to repair my broken jaw. I was fine about this surgery because I had already been through the neck surgery, and I was no longer scared. Before I was brought down for surgery, several phone calls were placed to the prep surgery room to make sure that all televisions in the room were turned off. I still didn't know that Chris and Deanna had not survived the accident. During my surgery, the surgeon repaired my jaw by inserting two permanent titanium plates. My parents were allowed to sit next to me in recovery, and although I have no memory of it, they sobbed the entire time.

It's all a blur to me, but I know that I was still asking for Chris. I was so worried about him, and I think that I somehow knew he wasn't okay.

By Tuesday, I was recovering from my surgeries and the decision was made to tell me the truth about Chris. One of my doctors wanted to be the one to tell me. He explained to my parents how he would go about it and what he would say. While my mom held my hand and my dad stood by, I was told that Chris, the love of my life, was gone. I was also told that my sweet, kind friend Deanna was gone as well. A therapist and a chaplain were in the room, but there wasn't much anyone could do. I was still very confused because I was on so much medication, and it was very difficult for me to process what I had just been told. I was devastated. I cried in disbelief, and my mom and dad cried with me.

Many of my family members and friends came to the hospital to see me. My grandpa even flew back from Florida as soon as he heard about the accident. Having so many people there to support me really helped a lot.

I remember looking at the fish that were painted on the ceiling in my hospital room, and I told one of my friends which fish was my favorite. I said that I had named the fish Chris. I was really focused on that fish named Chris.

My little cousins came to see me as well. My cousin Morgan, not quite five years old at the time, was very scared when she first saw me. She would not come near me. I had a neck brace on and my face and lips were swollen like a balloon. She hid behind my Aunt and blurted out, "She look scary, where's the doctor to fix her." That made everyone laugh.

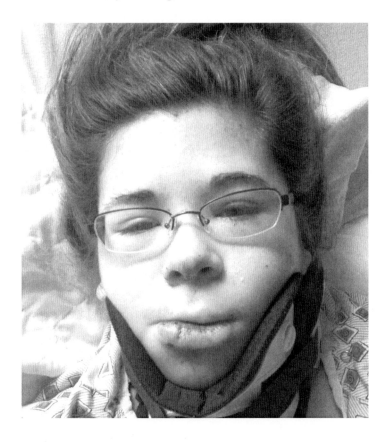

People came in my room that I don't remember at all. The Santa Express came in, and a man with a healing dog visited me as well. I was so surprised to hear they visited me because I had no memory of it at all. Countless kids from my school and friends of Matt's and Chris's came to the hospital hoping to see me. A lot of them didn't get a chance to because I was in the Pediatric Intensive Care Unit (PICU) and they had strict visitor rules. One of my friends caused quite a scene when she fainted outside my room and someone incorrectly paged a Code Blue. When my friend fainted, my grandfather was sitting with me and we were watching it through the glass doors of my room. My mom was down the hall on the phone with Chris's dad, watching as my dad held my limp friend in his arms. Hospital staff came running from all directions. My mom ran into my room and shut my curtains so I couldn't see what was happening because she thought it would upset me. In truth, I wanted to watch because this friend of mine always fainted. I knew she was okay but my mom had no idea. As this chaos unfolded, it added stress the PICU didn't need or want. It didn't come as much of a surprise when we were told that my friends were not allowed to visit me for the rest of the day!

The TV in my room was turned on once I was told about Chris and Deanna, and I watched Chris's parents being interviewed on Fox23 News. I was very groggy, and my mom said that I reached out to Chris's picture when it was shown on the television screen as if I could touch him. Her heart broke for me and for Chris. She loved him too and thought of him as a son.

During the interview, Chris's mom showed the necklace she was wearing. It was the cross that Chris was wearing the night of the accident. My entire family gasped, and I put my hand over my heart. It was the cross I had given Chris just days before the accident. It was a gift for our one year anniversary. That was such a painful moment.

We had no idea that the necklace had been recovered from the accident.

I also watched the candlelight vigil for Chris and Deanna from my hospital bed. I don't remember a lot of it because I kept falling asleep. The hospital had set up a big screen TV in my room, and my parents, grandfather, and some cousins were there visiting before the vigil came on. My pain medication was wearing off right before the vigil started, and I kicked everyone out of my room and I told my mother to turn the TV off. My mom was the only one left in my room, and she turned the TV on with the sound very low so she could hear Nikki speak. I remember telling her to turn it up when I heard Nikki's voice, so I was able to see Nikki make her speech on my behalf in front of thousands of people. It took a lot of courage, and she did such a good job. She loved Chris a lot, and I know he was proud of her.

The following day, I was able to visit with Matt. It was so good to see him, and I knew that he was the only one who could truly understand what I was going through. No one else was in the room with us during our visit and we were so tired we actually fell asleep while holding hands. My mom interrupted our visit to tell us there was a surprise for us. Matt was wheeled down the hall, and I walked down the hall with the assistance of a nurse. I started to cry as soon as I saw the surprise – some members of the Siena basketball team had come to the hospital to see us. I couldn't believe they were there. The guys told us that we were an inspiration to them, and my favorite player, O.D. Anosike, even gave a speech. They had signed Siena basketballs for both of us. After hearing about the accident, O.D had tweeted, "I get upset about losing games, meanwhile kids died on their way home from watching my games. What's more important? Pray 4 their families."

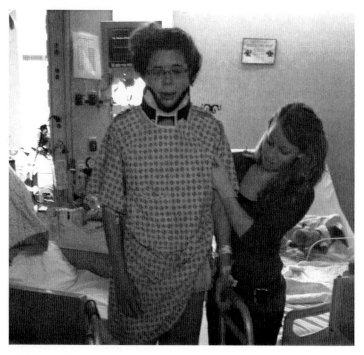

After their visit, O.D. tweeted, "Matt and Bailey told me they were my biggest fans. For the remarkable amount of courage they have shown, I'm their biggest fan also." O.D. will never know how much his support has meant to me, and I will be his fan for life. He continues to reach out to me even today. He says that he was deeply affected by the accident and that he now looks at life in a different way.

When the doctors told me I could go home after just a few days in the hospital, everyone was very surprised. They originally thought I would be there for at least two weeks. I was so happy to be going home. My parents were nervous; they were worried about my neck and concerned because I couldn't really eat anything. My neck surgeon said the best medicine for me was to go home. I never thought I was going to see my home again, so I couldn't wait to go home. There was only one problem: going home meant I had to get into a car. I was very afraid to get into a car because of the accident. I was crying, but my parents finally managed to convince me to get in. I was a nervous wreck and kept telling my dad to be careful. It's gotten a lot better since then, but being in a car still makes me anxious. My poor mom was so worried when I started driving again, but it was a big step for me to get back behind the wheel of a car. I'm more aware of bad drivers, and I am a more cautious driver.

When we pulled into our garage, there was a big sign on the inside garage door to welcome me home. My cousins and some of my friends were waiting for me, and our house was filled with flowers that people had sent. It felt good to be cared about by so many people. I was so happy my friends and family were there.

Although I was happy to be home, I was in terrible pain. There was a new bed and leather La-Z-Boy recliner set up for me so that I could stay in my parent's room. Because I came home sooner than expected, my grandpa had rushed out to buy the bed and the chair at the last minute. When he told the man at the La-Z-Boy store in Latham, NY who the recliner was for, they gave it to him for free. My grandpa said that both he and the manager of the store had tears in their eyes. My family has been overwhelmed by the love and support that has been extended to us by the community.

I had a dream about Chris on my first night home. I can't remember the details, but I woke up knowing that he had sent me a sign that he was okay in heaven. I continue to dream about him, and he seems to come to me on nights when I need comforting the most.

I have also been comforted by all of the support I have received from my friends and from the community. So many people have told me I am an inspiration to them. I don't really understand why they feel that way, but it's nice.

It still doesn't feel real to me that Chris is gone. Everything seems to remind me of him – movies, songs, commercials. New Year's Eve was especially difficult. Even though I was surrounded by my friends and family, I started bawling during the countdown. Chris and I had spent the previous New Year's Eve together and would have been together that night.

CHAPTER 2

||||||||||||||||||||||||||||||||||||||||||||||||||||||||||||||||||||||||||||||||||||||||||||||||||||||||||||||||||||||||

First Date

In October, 2011, I went to the Shen vs. Shaker football game that was taking place at Shen. I walked over to the Shen side of the stadium to say hi to two guys that I knew from diving. We took a picture of the three of us together, and one of the guys posted the picture on his Facebook. Chris was a friend of his and saw the picture and asked who I was. His friend told him about me, and Chris sent me a friend request on Facebook. Many people from Shen would send me friend requests, so I didn't think much of it.

Chris Stewart and Bailey Wind became friends.

October 29, 2011

After I accepted his friend request, Chris commented on one of my pictures. It was a picture of me, and his comment simply said "cute :)" I clicked like on his comment. Before long, we were chatting on Facebook and posting comments back and forth on each other's walls. After that, we exchanged numbers and started texting each other. I want to share some of our postings on Facebook when we started to get to know each other.

Chris Stewart and Bailey Wind
November 6, 2011

Chris Stewart

#that awkward moment when bailey sends you a kissy face when you didn't expect it.

Bailey Wind

#that awkward moment when chris stewart writes on ur wall....

Chris Stewart

#that awkward moment when bailey wind doesn't acknowledge that you have a sensitive side

Bailey Wind

#that awkward moment when chris stewart writes u a very deep paragraph

Chris Stewart

#that awkward moment when bailey wind keeps responding with

#that awkward moment when statements even though her and chris stewart are already txting

Bailey Wind

#the awkward moment when chris stewart realizes this is a awkward moment

Chris Stewart

#that awkward moment when bailey wind uses an "a" instead of "an" in her last "#that awkward moment when" statement.

Bailey Wind

#that awkward moment when chris stewart has to correct my grammer and also #that awkward moment when chris stewart didnt know what smh meant...smh

Chris Stewart

#that awkward moment when you txt me saying your in no class and i dont understand what you mean.

Bailey Wind

#the awkward moment when chris stewart texts me during prep which is a free period

Chris Stewart

#that awkward moment when chris and bailey always talk in third person for no reason.

Bailey Wind

#that awkward moment when i see one new text message from chris stewart and im scared to open it

Chris Stewart

#that awkward moment when bailey tries to tell chris she needs to go to bed but chris doesnt let her because he doesnt want to be lonely.

Bailey Wind

#that awkward moment that i almost just wrote that awkward moment on my homework because of chris stewart

Chris Stewart

#THAT AWKWARD MOMENT WHEN I COULDNT DOUBLE LIKE YOUR LAST #THAT AWKWARD MOMENT COMMENT!

Bailey Wind

#that awkward moment when chris stewart texts me saying.... ^_____^

Chris Stewart

#that awkward moment when chris looked at his phone and noticed his 69th txt came from bailey wind...

Bailey Wind

#that awkward moment when chris stewart likes all ur profile pictures and thinks hes cool cause i text him

Chris Stewart

#that awkward moment when bailey wind liked all of his profile pictures first, and texted him first

Bailey Wind

#that awkward moment when u told me last night to text u when i woke and now ur reputation is going to go up cause u talk to me

Chris Stewart

#that awkward moment when bailey wind is obviously lying because i do not remember telling you to text me first.

Bailey Wind

#that awkward moment when chris stewart feels the need to write on ur fb wall because he has nothing better to do

Chris Stewart

#that awkward moment when chris stewart is actually doing his algebra 2 homework while writing on bailey wind's wall and while texting her because he loves her.

Bailey Wind

#that awkward moment when chris stewart says that awkward moment when its really not that awkward

Chris Stewart

#that awkward moment when bailey wind says her phone is about to die but she miraculously is able to keep texting me the whole day.

Bailey Wind

#that awkward moment when chris stewart tells me his whole life story in 5 minutes

Chris Stewart

#that awkward moment when bailey wind texted me thinking she would win this awkward moment post challenge

Bailey Wind

#the awkward moment when i see that 100 people texted me and i pick chris stewart last to respond too

Chris Stewart

#that awkward moment when i chose to do a math problem before responding to bailey wind's ridonculous texts

Bailey Wind

#that awkward moment when i see that chris stewart texted me during class and i ignore it because i am trying to learn something new

Chris Stewart

#that awkward moment when bailey wind obviously didnt ignore it because she always texts back right away

Bailey Wind

#that awkward moment when chris stewart thinks i text him right away cause i dont, i have to respond to 100 ppl before him

Chris Stewart

#that awkward moment when bailey wind first met me by sending me a message saying, "i dont give boys my #, but here... (insert phone number here)

Bailey Wind

#that awkward moment when chris stewart embarasses me on facebook

Chris Stewart

#that awkward moment when i show my true love towards bailey wind by embarrassing her on facebook, and eventually in real life.

Bailey Wind

#that awkward moment when a notification pops up on my phone saying chris stewart also commented on his wall post and he texts me immediately after

Chris Stewart

#that awkward moment when a notification pops up on my computer saying bailey wind likes your comment, then also texts me immediately after as well.

Bailey Wind

#that awkward moment when u see that chris stewart is following u on twitter

Chris Stewart

#that awkward moment when bailey wind was the one to ask you to follow her on twitter first

Bailey Wind

#the awkward moment when christopher stewart told me a really funny story about oovoo

Chris Stewart

#that awkward moment when bailey wind likes over 100 things on my wall and gives me 122 notifications

Bailey Wind

#that awkward moment when chris stewart isnt acting like himself today

Chris Stewart

#that awkward moment when bailey wind wont tell chris whats different about himself

Bailey Wind

#that awkward moment when i dont know how to explain how chris stewart is acting differnet

The day after that random conversation, I found out that Chris was a Philadelphia Eagles fan. He found out that I was a Dallas Cowboys fan. I got this message and picture from Chris that day:

#that awkward moment when you were a cowboys fan and i was an eagles fan

I responded with this:

Tony Romooooooo<3333333333333333333333

As you can see, we did a lot of flirting! Going back and forth with our Facebook postings was a lot of fun.

We soon found out that we had mutual friends and that his cousin sat next to me in homeroom. Even though we learned a lot about each other through Facebook and texting, it was kind of strange to be texting someone I didn't know. I didn't want him to think I was creepy, so I pretended that I wanted to be fixed up with one of his friends. We laughed about that later!

One day my mom said, "Ummm, who is this Chris Stewart kid?" It was obvious that she had been stalking my Facebook wall, and I just told her that he was some kid from Shen. My mom noticed that he had posted something on my wall that mentioned that his cousin was a classmate of mine at Shaker. She recognized the name;

it was the name of the nephew of the woman who had bought my grandmother's townhouse two years earlier. My mom thought it was kind of weird and started to stalk Chris's Facebook wall. She would say, "Ask that Chris Stewart kid where he lives. I think he lives in grandma's townhouse." When I didn't ask him, she dug out the paperwork from the sale of the townhouse to find out the name of the buyer. It was Regina Stewart, Chris's mom!

I asked Chris about it, and sure enough, he had been living in my grandma's townhouse for two years. Before my grandma's death, she had lived there for almost thirty years. What are the odds of that happening? As I reflect back on that and remember how my grandmother was with me after the accident, I think she had something to do with the two of us finding each other. I believe that we were meant to meet. It was destiny.

In late November, Chris asked me to go to see a movie with him. I could play it cool and say that I wasn't excited, but that's not true. I was beyond excited! I was also very nervous and had only communicated with him by text and through Facebook. He had called my phone several times, but I had always been too nervous to answer. I didn't have any dating experience and was far from confident about the whole situation.

I was so nervous before our movie date. It was my first real date, and it would also be the first time we would meet in person. I was worried about it being awkward.

My mom brought me to the mall to meet him. I kept saying, "I don't want to go, I'm too nervous." She said that Chris was waiting for me and that it was too late for me to back out now. I'm so glad I didn't let my nerves get the best of me because I had a great time. Chris came out to the parking lot when I arrived and came over to my mom's car to meet her. He was so cute! He was wearing an orange polo shirt, jeans, and snapback. After he introduced himself to my mom, she said, "Oh my God, you are so adorable!" I couldn't believe she said that, and I told Chris that she was nuts.

We went into the movie theater to see Twilight Breaking Dawn Part 1 (even though I had already seen it) and Chris asked me if I wanted any popcorn or snacks. Of course, I said no. I was way too nervous to eat in front of him. In fact, I was so nervous that I sat through the entire movie with my arms crossed in front of my body. I was afraid he would try to hold my hand, and I didn't want him to feel how sweaty they were. He did have his hand on my knee though. At one point during the movie, he put his arm around me and put his snapback on my head. I put my head on his shoulder during a gross part. As we were leaving the theater, he asked me if he could hold my hand. I said no. My hands were way too sweaty. He later told me that he was nervous too, but he seemed a lot more comfortable than me. He never stopped talking, but that was good because it kept the conversation going. I thought he was kind of goofy but very cute.

We had our first kiss in front of the theater as we said goodbye. I hugged him, and he kissed me when I looked up at him.

His mom arrived to pick him up, so he said goodbye and went out to the parking lot to go home. When his mom found out that he had left me there alone, she sent him right back in to wait with me until my mom came. As we waited for my mom, I told him not to kiss me in front of her. I'm glad that he didn't think I was crazy.

After our first date, we chatted on Facebook and he said, "I guess we're dating now." And that is how it happened. That is how Chris became my boyfriend.

Here's what we posted after that first date:

Chris Stewart posted to **Bailey Wind**
November 27, 2011

Oh hey now it's our anniversary, I guess I love you?

Bailey Wind posted to **Chris Stewart**
November 27, 2011

love youuuuuuuuuuuuuuuuuuu<3

After that, we made it "Facebook official":

Chris Stewart and **Bailey Wind** started a Relationship

Chris Stewart
Cute 😊

Unlike · 👍 3 · More

CHAPTER 3

|||||||||||||||||||||||||||||||||||||||||||||||||||||||||||||||||||||||||||||||||||||||||||||||||||||||||||||||||||||||||||||||||||||||||||||

Welcome to the Nut House

The first time Chris came to my house, he was greeted at the door by my sister Nikki. She answered the door, saw Chris, and immediately shut the door in his face. Nikki thought she was being so funny. When I look back on it, I can't even imagine how awkward that must have been for Chris. He was nervous enough because he was coming to my house for the first time. That was just a preview of Nikki and her antics with Chris.

Nikki's friend PJ was at the house with her that day. They kept giggling and asking Chris a ton of questions. We watched a movie with them, but it was very awkward because Nikki and PJ were acting so silly. Chris chattered nervously, and I felt so bad for him. At one point, Nikki was acting crazy and jumped right on top of Chris. He excused himself to go to the bathroom after that, and he was gone for a very long time. My dad even noticed how long he was in the bathroom and asked what he could possibly be doing in there.

Poor Chris. As it turns out, Nikki had accidentally hit him in the crotch with her knee when she jumped on him. He was in terrible pain and felt as if he was going to throw up. That is why he was in the bathroom for so long.

After Chris left, I felt sure that he would never come back. I was very annoyed and embarrassed by the way that my sister had carried on. I couldn't even imagine what he must have thought.

As it turns out, despite the awkwardness of the situation and the inadvertent pain that Nikki had caused him, Chris said that he had a great time at my house. Really?? Chris came to love the energy and craziness of our house. There's a reason we have a sign hanging in our kitchen that says, "Welcome to the Nut House." Even my dad thinks we're all nuts. I'm glad that Chris embraced our nuttiness and that it didn't scare him away. He would always say, "You guys are great."

After that, it didn't take him long to become part of our family. He began to help himself to the refrigerator and snack cabinet. Chris would even text my mom and ask, "What's for dinner tonight, are we ordering out?" My mom loved how comfortable he became with her. In fact, it got to the point that she would be disappointed if she would come home from work and find that Chris was not there. Every time, she would say, "Is Chris coming over tonight?"

We always knew when Chris arrived. We would hear the double click of his car lock and then hear the sound of our refrigerator door ice machine. Chris always got a glass of ice water as soon as he walked in the door.

On his second visit to my house, Chris walked right over to my mom and gave her a hug before he left. I think he won her over with that hug; she certainly wasn't expecting it. My mom felt like he fit into our family so easily, and she looked forward to his visits. She eventually described him as the son she never had.

My dad liked him as well, and Chris always made a point to sit and talk to my dad when he came over to see me. He did the same thing with my mom. No matter where she was in the house, he would always find her to say hello. Both of my parents trusted him and even gave him the code to our garage door so he could let himself in if we weren't home. Sometimes he would be here when no one else was. He had his own spot in our finished basement, and we would find him there doing his homework or taking a nap. My parents even let him drive our cars so that he didn't always have to use up all of his gas.

My dad liked Chris right away because of his firm handshake and the way he looked him right in the eyes. My dad always teased Chris about leaving his swimming trunks on our pool fence, drinking "his" Pepsi, and always being in his way in the kitchen. It was always in jest because my dad loved Chris. My dad also use to say that Chris was always in the bathroom. After hearing him say that so many times, Nikki and I started telling Chris to go to the bathroom every five minutes when my dad was around. My dad would say, "Does he have some kind of a problem?" My dad wasn't in on the joke, but Chris, Nikki, and I thought it was hysterical.

We weren't the only ones in my family who loved Chris. Fenwick, my cousin, adored him. Fen is my aunt Doni's son. He is seven, and his sister, Morgan, is five. They live in Halfmoon, New York, so Chris and I spent a lot of time with them. Chris was always tickling Morgan, and I think she had a secret crush on him. Fen's adoration of Chris was no secret. He loved to play football with Chris, and he wanted to be just like him. He even started wearing the same kind of sneakers and socks as Chris. It was so cute! Fen loved to sit on Chris's lap and wear his hat. He and Morgan spent a lot of time with me and Chris in our pool. Fen loved it when Chris would throw him in the deep end. We had campfires, made crafts, and just had fun playing with the kids. Chris absolutely loved kids and looked forward to spending time with Fen and Morgan. Chris lovingly called Morgan, "Morgi the Monster." My Aunt Darcy's kids, Julius and Preston, loved Chris too but didn't get to spend as much time with him.

Fen was devastated after Chris's death, and he changed his baseball number to 69 which was Chris's football number. He also had the number 69 shaved into the back of his head. Fen may just be a little boy, but he and Chris were true friends. Chris always had time for him and was someone Fen could look up to; he was a wonderful role model.

Chris also made time to help my family whenever he could. I remember the time he sat at our kitchen table for several hours so that he could help my aunt Doni put together a slide show for a football banquet. Her knee popped out of place while they were working on it, so he went out to get an Ace bandage so that she could wrap it. He was always doing thoughtful things like that. He also painted a room in our house, moved furniture, and helped with our 2011 Christmas decorations. Nikki and I were responsible for decorating the Christmas tree with ornaments, but Chris ended up doing it for us. Every time he walked in the door, I would hand him the box of ornaments. As Christmas 2012 began to approach, Chris said to my mom, "I'm not putting the ornaments up this year. No way; they are not talking me into it this year. I don't care what they say." He said that over and over, but I know Chris would have hung those ornaments if he had been with us for Christmas. We couldn't bring ourselves to decorate our tree for Christmas 2012. We had a tree, but we hung no ornaments on it. It was decorated only with lights. My family has decided that our Christmas trees will look that way each year. Without Chris here to hang the decorations, we will go without them. It's our way of honoring and remembering Chris.

Chris was always there when you needed him. The time that we spent with my family was so full of love and happiness. We will treasure those happy memories forever.

CHAPTER 4

Rival Football Teams

When Chris and I met, we were both juniors in high school. Chris's football season had already ended for the year, so I did not get to see him play until the fall of 2012 when we were seniors.

Our high schools—Shen and Shaker— are major sports rivals. My family and I supported both schools long before I met Chris. My mom, aunts, uncle and cousins are all Shen graduates. Prior to dating Chris, we attended Shaker football games to cheer for my friend Schuyler. My parents are great friends with his parents, Kevin and Mia. Schuyler and I have grown up together.

When Chris joined our family, our excitement for football games reached a new level. We had always enjoyed going to football games, but now it was even better. We went to all of the Shen games and rooted for Shen. We would look forward to the games all week long; we couldn't wait to watch Chris play. My family would greet him at the gate as he exited the field after each game. Chris and I would always go to Friendly's after the game, and Nikki and some friends would join us.

One of Chris's biggest fans was my mom. She would always say that Chris was letting her relive her Shen high school football years. My mom would cut out every newspaper article that mentioned Chris—there seemed to be one every week. She would take a picture of it, put it on her Facebook wall, post it to Chris's wall, and then text it to him and his parents.

My mom received the following text from Schuyler's dad, Kevin, the week of the first Shen vs. Shaker football game;

Kevin:

Knock, knock, Shaker coming to knock Shen down

My mom:

Not with Chris Stewart on the line

Kevin:

Turncoat, traitor, Benedict Arnold

The day of the game, Kevin jokingly texted my mom that my parents better sit on the Shaker side or else. Kevin ran into Chris's dad before the start of the game in the parking lot, took a picture of them together and texted it to my mom. It said, "We are Family."

My parents decided that my dad would sit on the Shen side and my mom on the Shaker side. Prior to the game starting, my mom went on the Shen side to say hello to Chris's parents and jokingly told them she received "death threats" from her friends if she didn't sit on the Shaker side. Chris's dad had my mom put Chris's green jersey on. She got Kevin's attention from across the field, and she was dancing and waving at him while wearing Chris's jersey. Everyone laughed. My mom went over into the Shaker stands with the jersey still on. Everyone booed her and told her that they wouldn't talk to her unless she took the jersey off. It was all in good fun, and Shaker ended up winning the game.

The next night, Chris was at my house and we were all discussing the game. Chris explained that a few of the Shen starters didn't play at all because they were injured. He also said that some starters were playing at fifty percent because of injuries. My mom texted Kevin right away to tell him what Chris said. My mom loves to get Kevin going, especially when it comes to football. The two went back and forth with some funny texts, and we were still laughing about it when we heard loud pounding on our front door. We opened the door to find Kevin and Schuyler standing on the front porch pretending to be mad at us. It was quite a surprise and very funny; we had a lot of laughs about it. I took some great pictures that night of Chris in his Shen football t-shirt and Schuyler in his Shaker t-shirt. It made me happy that my boyfriend and my lifelong friend, rivals on the football field, became fast friends.

Shen played Shaker once again in the Super Bowl. Shaker won that game as well. My mom went to Kevin and Mia's house with a bunch of other Shaker parents after the game. Chris and I went out to eat. Later, Chris texted my mom to say we were coming over to hang out with them. That is an example of what I call a "Christopher moment." He was physically and emotionally beat up from the game, but he still wanted to go hang out with our Shaker friends. Chris was disappointed and depressed from losing the game, but he wasn't a sore loser. People meant more to Chris than sports.

Sports rivalry and competition will always exist, and it can be fun when it is kept in check. It should never be mean spirited or hurtful. Playing for different schools shouldn't automatically mean hatred toward each other as people. It was never that way for Chris. The friendship between Chris and Schuyler proved that sports rivals can become friends. That is how it should be. Why should where you live or where you go to school cause you to hate someone else? It just doesn't make any sense. Chris embraced everyone. He didn't care where you lived or what team you played for. He judged people based on their character. For Chris, rivalries existed only on the playing field. He was a true sportsman and treated even his rivals with respect.

Schuyler's dad, Kevin, sent my mom a text on the day after Shaker's Super Bowl victory. It read:

I got to tell you I think it took a lot for Chris to come over last night. Chris is a great kid and I am happy I got to know him. Schuyler and I were just talking about him as we were watching the game, he has a lot of respect for him. Too bad he couldn't have lived in Latham!!

Chris made that impression on everyone he met. I'm glad I am not the only one who got to experience "Christopher moments."

CHAPTER 5

My Christopher

Chris was 6'1", weighed 250 pounds, and was a lineman for the Shen High School football team. He was a leader on the field, and his high school teammates chose him to be one of their captains during his senior year. It would have been pretty easy for that to have gone to his head, but it didn't. He was popular, cute, smart, and athletic, but he never bragged or acted like he was better than anyone else. He would say hello to everyone. That's just the kind of person he was.

He loved to wear polo shirts, sweatpants, untied sneakers, and a baseball hat—backwards of course. You could always hear him coming because his huge, size fourteen sneakers made a lot of noise.

Chris was a big guy, but he didn't seem to pay much attention to his weight. I can only remember two times when it was obvious that his weight bothered him. The first time was in the winter of 2011 when we were at the first of many Siena basketball games together. At the Siena game that night, Chris became unusually quiet. It turns out that he was upset because he thought that people were probably wondering what a beautiful girl was doing with a fat kid. It broke my heart to hear him say that. I felt so lucky to have him as my boyfriend, and it didn't matter to me how much he weighed. I think his weight suited him, and I thought he was handsome. But I was not drawn to him because of his looks. I was drawn to him because of the person he was on the inside.

The only other time he acknowledged that his weight bothered him was the spring of 2012 when he went on a diet. We had been talking a lot about how we were looking forward to spending the summer in my backyard swimming pool, and he was determined to look good in his swimming trunks. Sure enough, he accomplished his goal and lost quite a bit of weight. I didn't think much about it at the time, but it must have been really hard for him because he loved to eat.

For the most part, Chris didn't spend too much time worrying about his weight. His frequent trips to McDonald's with his friends were legendary, and we were always going out to dinner together or with my family. Our favorite restaurant was the Recovery Room, but we also liked to go to Chili's, Fridays, Friendly's and 16 Handles.

The first time that Chris and I went out to dinner with my family was to celebrate his seventeenth birthday. We went to Friday's, and Chris ordered the three-course meal that included an appetizer, main meal and dessert. He ate every bit of it. He was one of those people who enjoyed every last bite of his meal. Then, when he was finally finished, he would lick his fingers. When I would see him do this, I always would say, "Chris!" He would just laugh and say, "What?"

One of our most memorable dinners was with my mom and Nikki at a fun restaurant in Boston, MA called Dick's Last Resort. Chris ordered an appetizer that included four different items. The waiter said, "Dude, that feeds 20 people!" As it turns out, it only fed one person, and that person was Chris. He ate the whole thing and probably licked his fingers when he was done.

At Dick's Last Resort, they give the customers paper chef hats. Your waiter puts the hat on your head after writing a funny insult on it. Mine read "Future MTV Star of Teen Mom" and Chris's read "She thinks I'm straight" with an arrow pointing at me. I still have those hats. We had so much fun that our waiter wouldn't let us leave; he wouldn't give us our check. We had the best time that night and enjoyed talking and laughing with our waiter and the other customers. We loved it so much that my mom was planning to take us back on December 15, 2012 as part of her Christmas gift to Chris. She was planning to get us tickets to a Bruins hockey game as well. The game never took place because of the NHL lockout, and our trip to Boston never happened because of the accident. Even though it makes me very sad that we weren't able to go back, I will always carry with me the happy memories from our wonderful night at Dick's Last Resort. And, of course, I will always treasure those paper hats!

Although we enjoyed going out to dinner, much of our time was spent at school and at sports practices. I am very serious about diving, and I devote a lot of time and attention to it. It's part of who I am. Because it is so important to me, Chris wanted to learn everything that he could about it.

Chris really wanted to see me dive, but I wouldn't let him come to one of my meets until many months after we started dating. The thought of him seeing me dive made me nervous; I don't know why but it did.

Chris kept asking to come to one of my meets, so I finally caved in and invited him to one at Harvard University. He was so disappointed when he found out that the first day of my meet coincided with a football tryout/day camp he was attending at the University of Massachusetts in Amherst. My mom came to the rescue and figured out a way for Chris to attend his camp and still make it to the second day of my meet. After Chris's football camp was over, we drove ninety minutes and met Chris and his dad at a McDonald's half way between the University of Massachusetts and Harvard. We then headed back to Boston, and Chris spent the night in the hotel with my family.

The next day, Chris finally got to see me dive. I texted him between all of my dives and told him if there was a dive I didn't want him to watch. If I thought I wasn't going to perform well on a particular dive, I certainly didn't want Chris to watch.

He sat in the stands with my parents and sister and asked my mom questions about every dive. It was all new for him, so he didn't understand the scoring or the difficulty ratings of individual dives. He was a quick learner and eager to learn everything he could about my sport. My mom said it was so cute to see how frustrated he would get with the judges when he disagreed with my scores. Anyone who is familiar with diving knows how he felt.

I ended up placing first in the Harvard meet, and I was so

happy that Chris was able to be there. From that point on, if he wasn't able to be at one of my meets, my mom would record each dive and send the video to Chris along with my scores. I would also text him after each dive. It felt so good to know that Chris was at the other end of his phone cheering me on. As he became more familiar with the scoring, he would get especially frustrated if he felt that the judges had "ripped me off" with their scores.

To say that Chris was supportive of my diving would be an understatement. He may not have always been able to be there in person at my meets, but it felt as if he was. I couldn't see him but I could feel his support. He could have been off enjoying his free time, but he was right there waiting by his phone so that he could experience every dive with me. He texted words of encouragement and helped me feel good about every dive no matter what I scored.

I remember one night when we laid on my backyard trampoline and Chris asked me about the numbers and letters associated with each one of my dives. He didn't just want to watch me dive; he wanted to understand everything about the sport. He asked so many questions that night, and it felt so good to lay there next to him. I realized how much he cared about my life and how lucky I was to have him as my boyfriend. I had always thought that teenage guys only cared about themselves, but not my Chris. He was not a self-centered person, and it was never just about him ever. His focus was always on me.

Chris took such an interest in diving that he asked me for some lessons. We used the diving board in our pool, and I later found out that he was also practicing at a friend's house. He was so excited when he mastered the back flip and couldn't wait to show me. How sweet is that? My boyfriend wanted to learn a dive just for me, and he secretly practiced so he could surprise me. My only regret is that I didn't capture his dives on video.

Chris was such an incredible boyfriend that I often ask myself, "How did I get so lucky? What was so special about me that Chris chose me?" I don't know the answers to those questions, but I do know that I could have never found a more special first love. I had no experience in the whole girlfriend/boyfriend stuff before I met Chris, but I managed to hit the jackpot on my first try. Chris was the sweetest, kindest, and most well-mannered and considerate boyfriend any girl could ever ask for.

Chris supported me in everything that I did, and I loved to support him as well. I may have made Chris wait to watch me dive for the first time, but he had no issues with me seeing him out on the football field. I would ask him if he ever thought about me watching him while he was on the field. He said that during the huddles he would think to himself, "Bailey's watching me. I have to do well."

Unlike Chris, I didn't find it necessary to learn the ins and outs of his sport. As long as I could see number 69 on the field, I was happy. I didn't spend time watching any other players. My eyes were always glued to 69. He played offense and defense and frequently played the entire game. I loved to wear his jersey and was proud for the world to see that number 69 was mine.

I hated to miss any of his games and only missed a few when I was out of town on official college visits. Chris totally understood; he knew that his football season coincided with the college recruiting time for my sport. He also knew that I would be thinking about him no matter where I was.

When I think back to Chris's football games, it was the two games that were played against Shaker that stick out in my mind the most. The first time that Shen met Shaker during the season, Chris suffered a high ankle sprain during the first quarter. After having to leave the field, he slowly limped up and down the sidelines in an attempt to get the pain to go away. When the injury prevented him from playing during the rest of the game, Chris was devastated. He sat down on the bench and leaned forward with his head in his hands. I have a heartbreaking photo of that moment. I can feel Chris's disappointment and anguish every time I look at it.

During halftime of that game, Chris was unable to walk to the locker room because of his injured ankle. He was left sitting on the bench alone, but not for long. I was able to go onto the field to talk to him. I have photos of the two of us by the bench in our number 69 jerseys. Those pictures are so special to me. When I look at them, I feel as if we are one—a perfect pair, a perfect team. It's just number 69 and his girl. Side by side, always there for one another.

Bailey Wind
I hope your ankle gets better Chris —
with Chris Stewart (remove)

Photos of You in Mobile Uploads · Sep 28, 2012 ·
Tag Photo · View Full Size · Make Profile Picture · Edit Photo · Hide from your timeline

When the team came out of the locker room, Chris stood up, hobbled past the benches, and extended his hand to greet each one of his teammates. That was so typical of Chris. Instead of feeling sorry for himself, he was there to support the rest of his team. It was another one of those "Christopher moments" I loved so much.

Shaker and Shen met once again at the end of the season for the Super Bowl. As the game progressed, it became apparent to everyone, including Chris, that the victory would belong to Shaker. Even though he knew they weren't going to win, Chris gave it his all until the very end. When the game ended, Chris was on his knees in the end zone. He had his head in his hands, and he was crying. My heart broke for him and I felt a huge lump in my throat. Eventually, Chris stood up and got in line to shake hands with the Shaker players. He was near the end of the line and kept his helmet on to hide his tears. I recently found out that Chris said to every Shaker player, "Bring it home boys". He was telling the Shaker football team to win the State Championship.

Chris and his teammates spent their final few minutes on the field hugging and crying in the end zone. The hugs were the type that seemed to last forever. I stood outside the fence with some friends and both of our families. I just stood and watched, hurting for him the whole time. At one point Chris left the end zone and walked to the 50 yard line. There he was, number 69, standing all alone on the 50 yard line at Sterwald Stadium. It was at that moment that I went to him. My 69 was no longer alone, and he cried on my shoulder as I hugged him. His high school football days had come to an end, and his pain was so visible on his tear-stained face. For him, it was about more than just losing the game. It was about saying goodbye to his beloved Shenendehowa High School football team. All of his years of hard work, dedication, and love for his teammates had come down to this moment. Chris would be one of the last players to walk off the field that night.

When I close my eyes, I can still see my number 69 standing there all by himself on the 50 yard line that night.

CHAPTER 6

The Brother She Never Had

Anyone who is close to me becomes friends with my sister, Nikki, and Chris was no exception. The three of us spent a lot of time together, and Chris and Nikki bonded very quickly. I have so many memories of the two of them together that it is hard to know where to start.

Chris was always making us laugh, and I will never forget the time that he squeezed into Nik's Victoria Secret yoga pants. She loves those pants and tried her hardest to be mad at Chris for stretching them out, but she just couldn't do it. How could she possibly be mad when she was laughing so hard at the sight of Chris in those yoga pants?

Nikki is a natural-born entertainer, and she loved to do crazy things to make Chris laugh. One day, she was dancing around in six-inch heels when she tripped and fell on top of Chris. He had just re-injured his ankle in a football game, and she landed right on top of it. Despite the fact that she caused him a lot of pain by falling on his bandaged ankle, he just laughed about it.

Every time she would see him, she would charge at him and yell "Ccccchhhhhrrrrriiiissss." She would then proceed to jump on top of him. When one of his mom's friends witnessed this, he asked, "Is that Bailey?" Chris replied, "No, it's her crazy sister." I can see why people may have thought that she was his girlfriend. She was always hanging off of him.

The three of us loved to play nightly volleyball games in our backyard. Chris and Nikki would join forces and play against me. They only beat me once, but they really savored that victory. From the way that they were jumping around and high-fiving each other, you would have thought they had won the Super Bowl!

Our long-haired German Shepard, Moose, kept a close eye on Chris when we were in the backyard. We call him Moose for a reason; he weighs 130 pounds. Moose didn't like it when Chris would give Nikki and I piggyback rides in the yard. He would run alongside of Chris and bite at him until he would have Chris's shorts down around his ankles. Nikki and I would fall to the ground and laugh hysterically, and Chris would just yell, "Moooooose!"

Nikki was always texting Chris, sometimes from the other room. When I was out of town for a diving competition, she would ask him to drive her to Hannaford or Target. Chris didn't exactly live down the street, and Nikki would beg and plead with him until he agreed to come over. He always ended up saying yes, and the truth was that he would have done anything for her. All that begging and pleading wasn't necessary, but it made it a lot more fun for him.

Nikki can be wild and crazy, but she can also be a "mother hen" at times. She was always checking my phone to read the text messages that Chris and I sent to each other. She wanted to make sure that there was nothing "inappropriate" going on. I ended up having to put a password on my phone to keep her from reading all of my messages. Nikki also worried about whether or not Chris's mom would be home when I went to his house. I think that it's sweet that she worried so much about me, but my mom had to remind her to give us space.

Chris and Nikki acted like brother and sister, and they had fun doing things to annoy each other. Chris enjoyed sneaking up on her when she was sunbathing; he would pick her up and throw her into the pool. Meanwhile, I remember the time that Nikki and her friends went to one of Chris's football practices with me. They kept screaming his name over and over; who does that? I'm sure he must have been really embarrassed, but he never complained. He was probably happy that she cared enough to want to come to his practice. Everyone called us his "little fans." What football player doesn't like having fans?

Nikki and I certainly added a lot of craziness to Chris's life, and he loved every minute of it. He used to say that we should have our own reality show and that he would watch it. During the quieter moments at our "nut house", Chris would sometimes paint our nails. Yes, you read that correctly. My lineman boyfriend would paint our nails and even help choose our colors! Chris was full of surprises.

Nikki tagged along with Chris and me on many occasions, but they also spent time together when it was just the two of them. They would come watch my diving practices at RPI and probably stop for some snacks on the way there. Chris and Nikki shared a love of food, and they were both always in the mood to get something to eat. Chris said that he could eat no matter how he was feeling, and Nikki felt the same way. Happy, sad, or tired, they were both always hungry. They would tease each other about it. I can't even count how many times Chris took us to Hannaford at night to buy snacks.

Most of all, Nikki just enjoyed spending time with
Chris. She appears in many of our pictures and wasn't
afraid of sticking herself right in the middle of any
shot. She also has plenty of pictures of just the two
of them. Chris never minded having Nikki around
and thought that she was funny and crazy. When she
would do some of her crazy antics, he would roll his
eyes, make a funny face, and say, "That's a damn Nikki
moment." He loved her like she was his little sister, and
she loved him like he was her big brother.

Nikki honored Chris by speaking on my behalf at the candlelight vigil that was held at Shen for him and Deanna. My fifteen-year-old sister managed to fight through her tears and address an enormous crowd at an overflowing football stadium. She spoke of her love for her one and only big brother. It was a beautiful tribute, and my whole family was very proud of her.

CHAPTER 7

Outside Forces

Do you believe in angels on earth? I do. Chris was one of them. I think that God puts these angels on earth for a reason. And then, when he feels they've done their job, God takes them back. Why else would God take my Chris from all of us who loved him so much? That is something that I will never understand.

Chris was a truly wonderful person, and I'm not the only one who knew that to be true. Chris wasn't just a great boyfriend and best friend to me. He was a great son to his parents, a great brother to his older brother Jeremy, a great "brother" to Nikki, and a great "son" to my parents. He was also a wonderful cousin, nephew, grandson, and friend. I could go on and on, but I think you get the picture. I know there is a television show called Everyone Hates Chris, but if it was about my Chris, it would have been called Everyone Loves Chris. I don't think I truly grasped the depth to which he was loved until after his passing.

Chris had a large circle of friends, and as I already mentioned, they loved him. There was less of Chris to go around after he started dating me, and this caused some of his friends to resent me. It's very difficult for me to write about this because it caused us both a lot of pain. But it is an important part of our story, one that I cannot leave out. Our relationship wasn't without its struggles; I call them "outside forces struggles." They came from outside of our relationship.

Chris had never had a serious girlfriend before me, so he had always spent a lot of time with his friends. That changed after I came on the scene. The fact that Chris had a girlfriend—one from a rival school—did not go over well with some of his friends. To say that they were not happy would be an understatement.

I never felt accepted as Chris's girlfriend. Although all of my friends quickly became Chris's friends, many of Chris's friends had no desire to become friends with me. I never quite understood why they disliked me so much. Maybe it was because I was from a different high school. Maybe it was because I was taking Chris away from them. Maybe it was because I spoke my mind and didn't let people push me around.

Being disliked by Chris's friends was especially hurtful to me because I felt as if I had never been given a chance. It wasn't the first time in my life that I had felt the pain of not being accepted; I even wrote my college essay on the subject. I would like to share it with you.

There's a Personality Under My Clothes

I never seemed to fit in or be accepted in elementary school. I was too young to realize why, or that it was because I looked different. I wore basketball shorts, crew neck t-shirts and sneakers. I had bangs and wore my hair in a ponytail. I didn't wear makeup. My girl classmates wore makeup, skirts, short shorts, tank tops and curled their hair. I was outgoing and involved in sports. Why didn't kids accept me? Why did my friends, all of a sudden, decide to not hang out with me? How I was treated during these years made me who I am, today.

The summer before middle school I was on a basketball team and met new girls. One teammate spent a lot of time at my house, but once school started she acted like she didn't know me. On two occasions she passed out Christmas goodies and invitations to a party in front of me and didn't hand me one. I sobbed to my mother that I had no friends and asked why no one liked me. During the school year I played on a different basketball team with girls who were all friends. They excluded me by not passing me the ball and moving their seats when I sat with them. Sometimes, on the way to practices and games I cried because I felt so alone. It was difficult staying in situations like that, but I never quit, and I never changed who I was.

As I entered high school I began to change on my own. I wore more girlish clothing, grew my bangs out and wore my hair down. Some students didn't recognize me. I received compliments on my appearance, but my friend situation didn't improve. I had casual conversations with and said hello to kids, but I didn't have friends to hang out with. During the first school football game I attended I sat with my mom because kids I approached walked away with their friends. In my junior year I was accepted into a "group" when girls who sat at my lunch table saw me at another game and thought I was funny. They were able to see my personality.

I never changed for anyone. I will not do something I think is wrong just to be accepted. All of these experiences have made me into the person I am, one who can go into any situation without knowing anyone, who won't change her beliefs just to be accepted, one who knows what it is like to not have any friends and who will reach out to someone sitting alone; and who accepts people for who they are and not how they look.

I shared this essay to give you a glimpse of who I am. I'm sure that many people will be surprised after reading it. After the accident, people saw pictures of me on the news and heard that I would be diving at the University of Tennessee. They also learned that I was dating a very popular football player. Wow! Sounds like a girl with a lot of self-confidence, doesn't it?

In truth, I have always struggled with self-confidence.

Since the accident, many people have told me that I am beautiful. I have never seen myself that way. My mom would tell me over and over that all girls my age struggled with image, looks, and confidence issues. But did I listen to her and believe that she was speaking the truth? Of course not. After all, I am a teenager!

Chris helped me a lot with my self-esteem issue, and he made me feel beautiful and secure. But the fact that his friends disliked me chipped away at my self-confidence. I wondered what was wrong with me that caused them to dislike me so much. It made me feel unworthy and hurt me deeply.

I wasn't just imagining that Chris's friends didn't like me. I wasn't being overly sensitive or taking things too personally. They made their feelings perfectly clear. Some of them documented these feelings in hurtful twitter and text messages. Although I have copies of the messages, I have decided not to share them publicly. What good would it do? I am not looking for revenge or trying to hurt anyone. But I am also not going to gloss over it and pretend that it didn't happen. But it did happen, and it was extremely hurtful to me and to Chris.

One of Chris's friends made it very obvious that she didn't like me from the first time she met me. No matter how many times we saw each other, she barely acknowledged that I existed. She even sent some terrible text messages about me to Chris. I have copies of them because Chris shared them with me. She felt that I had changed Chris and had taken him away from his friends. She missed the times they all hung out as friends. She wanted to go back to the way things were and wanted me out of the picture.

Needless to say, I began to dislike her. She was saying unkind things about me to my boyfriend, yet she had never taken the time to get to know me. She believed I was in the way of their friendship, and she was punishing me because of those feelings. Chris expressed his displeasure for the way she was treating me, but it didn't change anything. She would take pictures of Chris from a distance and add smiley faces and kisses to them before posting them on the internet. I just couldn't understand why she was doing this.

I wish that I could say this was the only problem that I had with Chris's friends, but it was not. As Chris's junior prom approached, I asked if there was room on the prom limo bus for one of my Shen friends. I was not aware that the group with whom we were going with didn't care for my friend and didn't want her on the bus. Chris was told that there would be "no room" for my friend and her date in the group picture either. The whole situation ended up causing trouble—trouble that I didn't need. It was just another strike against me in the eyes of Chris's friends.

Most of the girls on the limo bus were friends with the girl who disliked me. None of the girls knew me, but it was obvious that they had made the decision not to like me. So there I was on prom night. On a limo bus surrounded by people who didn't want me there. While on the bus, one of Chris's male friends started talking about one of my Shaker friends. He spoke loud enough for us to hear. This made me even more uncomfortable, and I couldn't understand why he was saying these things. I spoke right up and said, "Could you please just stop." The whole bus went quiet. It's not what I had dreamed of for my prom night. Chris and I did not let all that happened on the bus interfere with our night together. We danced, took pictures, and had a wonderful time together. Unfortunately, the night took a turn for the worse after the prom ended. We went to a party with Chris's friends, and I felt very unwelcome. Chris could sense it as well and told me that he would understand if I left. I called someone to come pick me up and left as quickly as possible. After I was gone, some of the girls told Chris they were glad I had left. Chris got so upset that he ended up leaving the party a short time later. He texted my mom at 2 A.M. to tell her what happened and how upset he was about it.

It is still so hurtful to me when I think back on that night. Those girls didn't even know me. They met me for the first time that night. What could I have possibly done to make them treat me so badly? I was hurt and humiliated, and I came home and cried my eyes out to my mom.

After the prom, Chris began receiving more and more nasty text messages about me. These messages hurt Chris just as much as they hurt me. The behavior of some of his friends embarrassed and disappointed him. He had never been in a situation like that and didn't know what to do. Chris was caught in the middle.

I believe that his friends were doing all of this to break us up. That didn't happen. In fact, our relationship grew even stronger because of what we went through together.

Feeling unwelcome at the prom was nothing compared to what happened to me at one of Chris's football games that took place at Shen. I would always wear his number 69 jersey with pride, and the sight of me wearing his jersey did not make everyone happy. At every game, some Shen kids would stare, glare, and whisper when I walked by. At this particular game, I directed a greeting at some of the kids in the Shen section. What happened next wasn't pretty. My greeting was misinterpreted as a rude gesture, and some nasty remarks flew back and forth between some Shen students and the friends I was with. After being taunted, I was followed by three male students. They told me that a Shen girl—the friend of Chris's that I already had problems with— wanted me to know that Chris was cheating on me with her. They told me that they had witnessed the two being affectionate in the halls at school. Of course, I didn't believe them. But I did have a total meltdown, and I ended up crying. If you are wondering why I even tried to say hi to the kids in the first place, I was just following some advice that I had received. Someone told me that being friendly might improve my situation. Oh well, so much for advice!

A Shen parent who was in the stands saw me being bullied, and he took action. Although I had never met him before, he came to my aid. At the end of the game, the same man pulled Chris aside and told him what had happened. I will forever be thankful to him for being so kind to me. He has been part of my life since that night. Maybe he's one of those angels on earth that I believe in.

Chris received a lot of text messages later that night. I probably don't have to tell you that the messages weren't very nice and that they were about me. People were telling him versions of what happened in the stands, and these versions were nothing like what had actually happened. The fact that a Shen parent— someone who didn't know me— witnessed what was happening and felt compelled to intervene on my behalf speaks for itself. I would not be honoring Chris's memory if I wasn't being honest about what happened that night.

The text messages continued to pour in to Chris, and some of my haters began to vent about me on Twitter. I wasn't named in any of the mean tweets, but it was obvious to both me and Chris that they were about me. There was one very cruel tweet that was obviously about me, and it was sent directly to Chris. Chris repeatedly asked his friend to delete the tweet, but he wouldn't. I was very upset and humiliated.

I remember how Chris sat on my mom's bedroom floor that night and read all of the text messages to us. One friend texted him and said, "It's her or me." Another friend of Chris's – one of the few that I thought actually liked me – tried to convince Chris that I was the one who had started the trouble at the game and that I was trying to blame others. My heart sank yet again. It was especially painful because I thought he was my friend too. Plus, he wasn't even there to witness what took place in the stands. He heard about it at a party and immediately sided against me. Looking back on it, his behavior shouldn't have surprised me. He had always made it seem like we were in a competition for Chris's attention. After the accident, he visited me in the hospital and spoke to my mom. He told her that he had addressed what he referred to as "The Bullying of Bailey." My mom was shocked to hear those words come out of the mouth of someone who had actually been part of the bullying problem. It made her very uncomfortable, but as far as she was concerned, none of that mattered anymore. She knew that she had to focus on moving forward and forgiving those who had treated me so badly. Although she has done a great job of doing that, she can still hear those words in her head: "The Bullying of Bailey." Those four words acknowledged what we already knew. I had been bullied. He knew it, and so did we.

On the evening that Chris received those tweets from his friends about me, he ended up becoming so upset that he left his phone in my mom's bedroom while we watched a movie downstairs. It was all so hard on Chris. The situation was really becoming out of control. Neither of us knew what to do.

I have to wonder if anyone thought about Chris's feelings during all of this. I have so many questions.

Did his friends ever stop to think about how their actions were affecting him?

Could they not see that they were causing him pain?

Why were people taking sides when they weren't in the stands to witness what happened?

What gave them the right to try to destroy our relationship?

Why didn't Chris's happiness matter to them?

As hard as it is, I have to come to terms with the fact that I will never know the answers to these questions. I try to make sense out of all of it, but I know I never will.

The next day, I received a message from a Shen girl who was in the stands with the kids that taunted me at the game. She wanted to let me know how terrible she felt. She apologized to me for what those kids did to me and said that I didn't deserve it. Her message meant a lot to me.

The very next night, things began to get bad again.

Some people who I don't even know—family members of the girl who was causing so many problems for me—started tweeting terrible things directly to me. They just wouldn't stop. What was said was so bad that my parents called the police to our house that night at 1:00 A.M. I have chosen not to share the tweets publicly, but they were shown to the police.

After speaking with the police and thinking things over, my parents decided to hold off on filing the police report. We decided that I should shut down my Twitter until the whole situation blew over. As all of this was happening, Chris was asleep in our basement. He was totally unaware of what was unfolding upstairs. We had to wake him up so that he could come talk to the police; what a shock that must have been for him.

Chris was not a person who liked conflict, so he didn't confront anyone about the situation. He didn't know what else to do, so he just continued with his week at school like nothing happened. I don't know why, but Chris chose not to tell his parents about what was going on. He felt he could handle it, and I know he was hurt, torn and confused.

I admit that I did not always handle the situation as well as I could have. There were times when I said something I shouldn't have or reacted in a way that may have made things worse. But I can assure you that I never wrote anything hateful about anyone else; I only defended myself. In my opinion, bullying someone online is one of the cruelest and most humiliating things you can do to a person. Cyber bullying is also against the law. If it ever happens to you, make sure to do what I did. Keep copies of all of the messages before they are deleted.

A week before the accident, Chris said to me, "I'm going to get my friends to like you."

My response was, "How are you going to do that?"

He didn't have an answer for me at the time. But Chris always kept his promises.

The night before our accident, there was another incident at a Shen event. This time Chris was sitting right next to me. He witnessed the whole thing. There was no way for anyone to twist things and place the blame on me this time. Chris told me we were leaving. He was so upset on our drive back to my house that his voice was cracking. He had finally had enough. After everything that we had been through, he had reached his breaking point.

About twenty-four hours later, the love of my life was gone. After his death, his friends rallied around me. Some have apologized. Some have cried with me.

Chris was right. He was able to get his friends to like me. Sadly, it took his death to accomplish this. It was what he always wanted, and I know he is happy about it. I just wish he was here to see it. I told you that he always kept his promises.

As I reflect on this very painful part of our love story, I want to stress again that it is not my intention to hurt anyone. But this is such an important part of our story, and I cannot pretend it didn't happen. Describing this situation also proves how deeply we loved one another. There is no other way that we could have stayed together through all of this. We may have been only 17 years old, but our love for each other was strong.

I have no hard feelings or hold any grudges. All that I am capable of feeling these days is love for Chris and the aching pain caused by living life without him. To those who have hurt me in the past, I thank them for the kindness they showed me after Chris's death. It truly means a lot to me, and I know that Chris would be proud of the way his friends have acted towards me. I hope that things stay as they are now with everyone. That is what Chris would have wanted.

Through all of this, I continue to be plagued with self-doubt. I ask myself, "Did I deserve for this to happen to me? Did I do something wrong?" I wonder if every teenager who has been bullied asks themselves these questions. It is important for anyone who has been bullied to acknowledge that the behavior of a bully is a reflection on them, not on you. Many bullies don't characterize their behavior as bullying even when it clearly is. I found that to be true of many of the people who bullied me. I can only hope that reading my story will open some eyes. The effects of bullying are devastating, and it causes tremendous harm.

My cousin told me that he was in line at Chris's wake and overhead the conversation of the Shen students who were standing behind him. They were talking about how badly Chris's friends had treated me and what "jerks" they must have felt like at that moment. Part of me feels vindicated by their words. But other parts of me continue to think that there must be something wrong with me— why else would they have treated me that way?

I don't ever want things to go back to the way they were before. I want Shen and Shaker to stay united forever as a tribute to Chris and Deanna. I want for acts of goodness and kindness to continue to occur in their memory. I want people to think twice before hurting another person. I want everyone to treat others the way Chris and Deanna did – with incredible kindness. Most of all, I want people to remember the legacy that Chris and Deanna have left behind. They were amazing human beings and everyone should learn and live by their example. That includes me.

CHAPTER 8

||||||||||||||||||||||||||||||||||||||||||||||||||||||||||||||||||||||||||||||||||||||||||||||||||||||||||||||||||||||||||||||||||||||||||||||||||||||

A Walk to Remember

About a week before the accident, on November 23, 2012, Chris and I watched the movie A Walk to Remember. My aunt knew about the troubles that we were experiencing, and she suggested that we watch it. I cried through the whole movie, and Chris even got choked up. Later that night, he tweeted:

I've never seen a better movie in my entire life, most inspirational thing ever #AWalkToRemember

Can you picture a 250 pound lineman saying that about a "chick flick?" It proves what I already knew; Chris was a gentle, sweet soul.

If you have never watched the movie, Landon and Jamie are the main characters. They face many challenges in their relationship, and their love for one another is tested. Landon is very popular, and his friends do not want him dating Jamie. His friends do terrible things to publicly humiliate her. Landon ends up choosing his relationship with Jamie over his relationship with his friends. Jamie's death from cancer at the end of the movie leaves Landon devastated.

After we watched the movie, I started calling Chris Landon and he called me Jamie. Chris felt he learned a lot from the movie. He said that it was going to help him handle situations differently in the future. A few days later, we got up and left when some of his friends mistreated me at a Shen event. I felt like it was a turning point for him, and I believe it occurred because of the movie.

On the way to the Siena basketball game on December 1, 2012, I told Deanna about the movie and shared how much it had affected Chris. Deanna was very curious and kept asking Chris why it had made such an impact on him. I told her that she needed to watch it with Matt.

The day after I found out that Chris had not survived the crash, my mom said, "Chris is your Walk to Remember." I cried and said, "Why did you have to say that?" But she was right. Landon and Jamie had a special love for one another that ended way too soon. Chris and I had a special love that ended way too soon as well. I am thankful he didn't die alone. I was right there by his side— just like Landon was beside Jamie when she died.

It is surreal when I think about it. Just a week before Chris's death, I was watching that movie and crying tears for two fictional characters. A short time later, I was crying my own tears filled with pain and loss that was all too real.

Chris and I may have only been 17 years old, but we were in love. I wanted to spend every minute of every day with Chris. We texted every night before we went to bed, and we texted every morning when we woke up.

I couldn't wait to get out of school every day so that I could see him. We didn't even have to be in the same room. Sometimes I'd be in one room doing homework and he'd be in another room at my house doing homework. It didn't matter as long as we were together. He would stay at my house until the last possible minute and was often late getting home. It always took us awhile to say goodbye. Sometimes Nikki was involved in the goodbyes too; she would still be jumping on him as he headed out the door. He texted me as soon as he got home. Sometimes he even texted my mom because he knew that she worried about him too.

Chris was my best friend. I thought about him every minute of every day; I still do. If that isn't love, then what is? I don't think I am too young to know what love is. I can't say that I know what would have happened in our future, but we did commit to each other to stay together through college. We talked about getting married after we graduated. We were determined to make going to different colleges work. It may sound silly to some people, but it wasn't to us. A lot of high school sweethearts end up getting married. Those were our dreams, and we believed they would come true. That is all that mattered.

We will never know what could have been, but I do know one thing for sure. Chris will be a part of my life and my family's life forever.

CHAPTER 9

‖‖

Deanna

I met Deanna at the Shen junior prom in May 2012. She and Chris were good friends and had a lot of classes together. The day after prom, Deanna wrote on my Facebook. She said that Chris and I were so cute and that she was glad she finally met me. Chris gave me Deanna's cell phone number, and we started texting one another. Deanna would take pictures of Chris in school and forward them to me. I thought that was so cute. Eventually, we started sending pictures back and forth to one another. That was the beginning of our friendship.

Chris and I were at his house one night when Deanna texted him and asked if we wanted to come over and hang out with her and Matt. The four of us had a great time talking and taking pictures of each other. We had so much fun together, and that night marked the beginning of my friendship with Deanna. She was so sweet, and she liked me. One of Chris's friends actually liked me! It was a great feeling.

Our friendship continued to grow, and Chris, Nikki, and I went to one of Deanna's softball games. Nikki and I became friends with Deanna's little sister, Jenna. Jenna would paint my nails when I was at her house. Deanna and I would take trips to Cumberland Farms to get milkshakes and hot fries. Sometimes we would just drive around, talking and listening to music. We really enjoyed just spending time together.

The first time all four of us went out, we went to a
carnival in Clifton Park. We had a lot of fun playing the
games; we didn't go on any of the rides because we were
too afraid they would break! We played one game that
involved a water squirter. Deanna won the game, and her
prize was a big giraffe. Instead of taking her big prize, she
asked if she could have two smaller ones. She gave one of
them to me. That's how thoughtful she was. We went out
for ice cream after that then back to Deanna's house to
watch a movie.

Chris and I hung out a lot with Deanna and Matt during
the summer of 2012. When we were at Deanna's, we
would hang out in her basement. One of my favorite
memories involved the four of us playing Just Dance.
Can you guess who the best dancer was out of the four of
us? It was Chris! Matt would get tired or frustrated and
end up taking a rest. Chris didn't need to take a break. He
never got tired of dancing.

When I look back on the time that we spent together as couples, I feel very lucky. We had so much in common and really enjoyed hanging out. I remember how we all used to fall asleep while watching movies together at Deanna's. It got to the point where Deanna and I knew to set an alarm for midnight. Chris and Matt would leave, and Chris would drop Matt off at his house.

Deanna and I spent time together when it was just the two of us. Our friendship wasn't restricted to double dates. The first time Deanna came to my house, we hung out by my pool. We had so much fun that she said she wanted to hang out at my house every day during the summer.

At one point, Deanna and I were obsessed with making friendship bracelets. We spent a lot of time trying to make them, but we always failed at it.

During August 2012, Chris and Matt lifted weights each morning with the football team. After they were done, they would come over to my house. Deanna would already be there from the night before. We would all fall asleep for a nap, and then Chris and Matt would make breakfast. Matt once placed an entire package of bacon in a pan and started cooking it in one big chunk. We all laughed, and Chris ended up showing Matt how to cook bacon that morning.

We would spend the rest of the day relaxing by the pool. We lounged on the lawn chairs or on the floats. Matt would sometimes pull Deanna into the pool; she didn't want to get her hair wet and wouldn't get in on her own. I have such nice pictures of those days of the four of us together.

When Deanna and I were getting ready for football season, we took a trip to the craft store. We bought a lot of supplies and made signs for our boys. Sometimes we would sit together at the football games. I liked to walk around and Deanna liked to sit up in the stands. She would get so excited when Matt would play. She would shake me and say, "Matt's in, Matt's in."

Deanna and I didn't get to see each other as much during the football season. The boys were busy with practice and games, we all had our school work and I had my diving practice. Deanna would always try and plan a time for us to get together, but it was tough in the fall of 2012. We were able to squeeze in a sleepover a couple of weeks before we went to that Siena basketball game.

Before leaving my house on December 1, 2012 to go to the basketball game, Chris, Deanna and I talked about what happened at the Shen event the night before. Shen basketball season was about to begin, and Deanna suggested that Chris and I come to the basketball games with her. She said we'd have no problems there and that we'd have fun together. We all agreed that it was a great idea. Deanna didn't hang out with the kids who had been cruel to me, and she always felt bad about what I was going through. It helped a lot to be able to confide in her about it. I look back and realize how smart she was to sit in another section at the football games, a section far away from the kids who caused so many problems for me. I should have sat there with her every game.

I can understand why Chris was such good friends with Deanna. The two of them had similar qualities. I feel so fortunate that she was my friend and that she gave me a chance. Deanna gave me a chance!! She didn't prejudge me, and she didn't form an opinion of me based on someone else's. Deanna took the time to get to know me as a person. I love her for that.

I will miss how sweet, friendly and kind hearted Deanna was. I will miss how she used to always go up to my mom, hug her, say "you're crazy," and then laugh. I will miss her smile, which was always on her face. I will miss seeing how happy she always was. I will always treasure the special memories of the times the four of us spent together. They are some of the best memories of my life. For me, Deanna's light will always shine bright like a diamond.

CHAPTER 10

Chris's Words

Can you feel Chris's kindness through the words I've written? Are you getting a sense of his incredible personality? I want you to. If you didn't know Chris, I want you to feel like you did. I want you to feel his goodness. I want you to hear his own words from his heart so you can really know him. This is his story too, and I want you to hear some of his words.

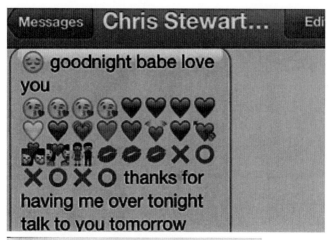

Chris gave me the sweetest card for Valentine's Day, a big box of chocolates, a balloon, earrings, flowers, and a stuffed gorilla. The gorilla was holding a frame that contained a picture of Chris when he was little; it was the cutest thing ever!

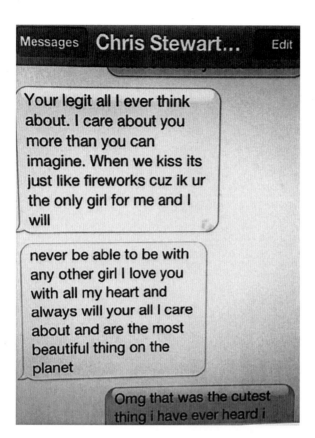

Messages **Chris Stewart...** Edit

Your legit all I ever think about. I care about you more than you can imagine. When we kiss its just like fireworks cuz ik ur the only girl for me and I will

never be able to be with any other girl I love you with all my heart and always will your all I care about and are the most beautiful thing on the planet

Omg that was the cutest thing i have ever heard i

Messages **Chris Stewart...** Edit

It's weird cuz I've always dreamed of being in that situation. Holding my girlfriend, crying, in my arms telling her everything will be ok. It's weird and idk why but tonight I lived that dream 🖤

Chris had a whole wall in his room that he dedicated to me. He hung up every card I gave him along with all of the drawings we made together. We used to sit at my kitchen counter and color and draw together!

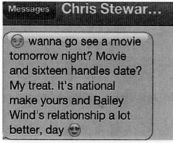

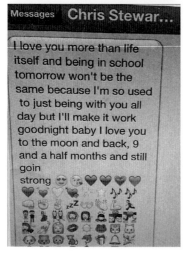

Chris Stewart
@Stewz77

You're so beautiful, so dam beautiful <3

On black Friday, Chris surprised me and showed up at Ihop while I was having breakfast. He had a card and flowers and told me that he was coming shopping with me.

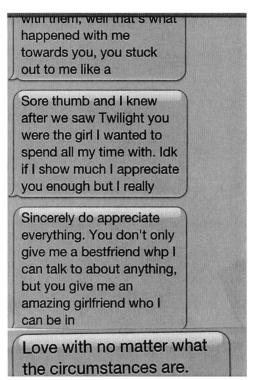

with them, well that's what happened with me towards you, you stuck out to me like a

Sore thumb and I knew after we saw Twilight you were the girl I wanted to spend all my time with. Idk if I show much I appreciate you enough but I really

Sincerely do appreciate everything. You don't only give me a bestfriend whp I can talk to about anything, but you give me an amazing girlfriend who I can be in

Love with no matter what the circumstances are.

You're the only person I want to see myself with and I will do whatever it takes to keep it that way. I love you

More than I love myself basically and I never want anything to come between us <3

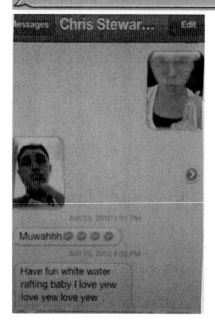

Chris Stewar...

Muwahhh

Have fun white water rafting baby I love yew love yew love yew

stewz77 Txts I get from @bailswindy while she's in myrtle. She's the best and I love her and wish she would come home 🖤🖤🖤🖤🖤🤍🤍🐢😸

Chris would always sing to me in the car. Most notably, the song Wanted.

Chris Stewart
@Stewz77

@BaileyWind kickin ass in #TN

6/26/12, 11:13 AM

Chris Stewart
@Stewz77

Shout out to the world's greatest girlfriend @BaileyWind happy 6 months babe it's been the best half year of my life I love you 🤍🖤🤍🖤🖤🖤

5/27/12, 1:41 AM

137

Chris Stewart
@Stewz77

With my bitches @BaileyWind and
Deanna Riverzzz

5/25/12, 11:26 PM

Chris Stewart
@Stewz77

Very successful date night with
@BaileyWind

Chris Stewart
@Stewz77

#That1Friend that can be your
girlfriend and bestfriend that you
can tell everything too, and act
yourself around them
@BaileyWind

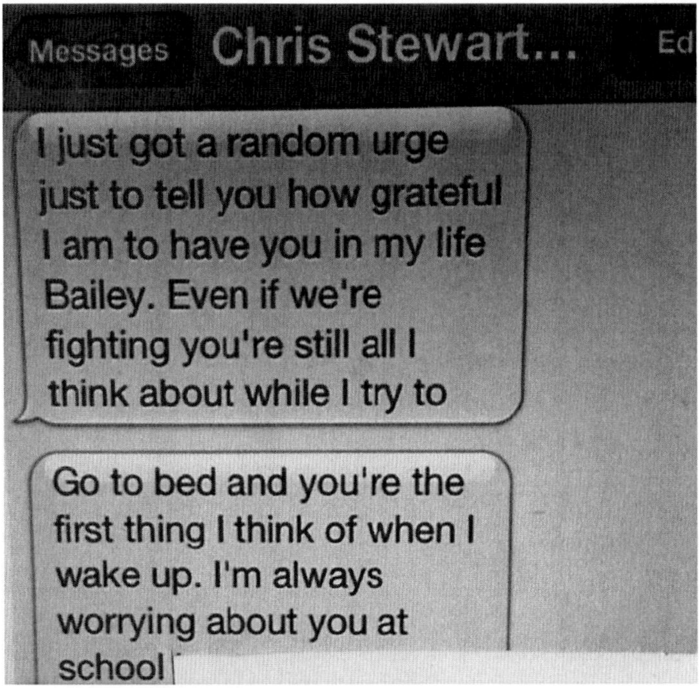

Messages **Chris Stewart...** Ed

I just got a random urge just to tell you how grateful I am to have you in my life Bailey. Even if we're fighting you're still all I think about while I try to

Go to bed and you're the first thing I think of when I wake up. I'm always worrying about you at school

Chris Stewart
@Stewz77

Falling asleep listening to you da one, #sotrue #youAREtheonlyone

Chris Stewart
@Stewz77

#Flirting with @BaileyWind
>>>>>>>>>>>

Chris Stewart
@Stewz77

Watching Twilight was good
enough, but it made it better since
I was with @BaileyWind <3

Chris Stewart
@Stewz77

My girlfriend > your girlfriend

8/13/12, 1:36 AM

Just before our first year anniversary, Chris recreated
our first date night. When I showed up at the mall, he was
wearing the same outfit he wore on our first date. I now
have that shirt he wore. He videotaped me as I walked
toward him. Yes, I was embarrassed, I covered my face.

Chris Stewart
@Stewz77

Girl you're amazing just the way
you are

8/3/12, 5:17 PM

Chris Stewart
@Stewz77

We might be thousands of miles
away but we are still together☽

8/4/12. 10:24 PM

Chris made it a routine of buying me a pair of socks from
every college he visited. I, in return, bought him t-shirts
from every college I visited.

Chris Stewart
@Stewz77

Good luck at nationals tomorrow
@BaileyWind I love you #killit
#flipnrip ♥♥💦💨☘️🐵●●●
👕👗

Chris Stewart
@Stewz77

@BaileyWind come home soon

7/13/12, 12:45 PM

When I would get home from some of my diving competition trips, Chris would always have surprise presents and cards waiting for me on top of my bed.

Chris Stewart
@Stewz77

"@ShitGuysDntSay: I love you sugar plum" @BaileyWind hahahaha #insidejoke

7/2/12, 7:49 AM

Chris Stewart
@Stewz77

@BaileyWind I MISS YOU MORE

6/21/12, 11:54 PM

Chris Stewart
@Stewz77

@BaileyWind she spoils me 😏 #candy pic.twitter.com/KhFNIJ7ι

7/31/12, 3:22 PM

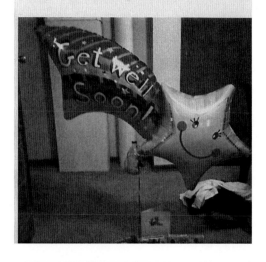

stewz77
I love you💜

deannarivers
I LOVE HER 🖤

bailswindy
@deannarivers @stewz77 I LOVE YOU BOTH🖤

Chris Stewart
@Stewz77

Happy birthday @BaileyWind love
you

10/18/12, 6:33 AM

Chris Stewart
@Stewz77

#EaislyAttractedTo @BaileyWind

10/8/12, 8:00 PM

Chris Stewart
@Stewz77

Spent a great day with
@BaileyWind apple picking and
hanging with her little cousins

Chris Stewart
@Stewz77

Congrats @BaileyWind for
committing to Tennessee for
diving, so proud of you and I know
I'll see you in the Olympics one day
#Vols

Chris took pictures and videos of my mock Letter of Intent signing day at Shaker High School. He always told me how proud he was of me and he stood there watching me get interviewed with such a look of pride.

Chris Stewart
@Stewz77

#MentionSomeoneWhoWillCompl
eteYourDay Bailey Wind

For our one year anniversary, Chris took me to his room and told me I couldn't go downstairs. When he was ready, he covered my eyes and guided me down the stairs. He had nice music playing and candles on the table. Chris had all of my favorite foods: mozzarella sticks, McDonald's French fries (I love French fries), and a Dunkin Donut bagel. He gave me a black diamond infinity ring, and I gave him a cross necklace. We went to Friendly's to finish the night off, and Chris ordered a 1,000 calorie ice cream.

After Chris's passing, his mom came across an essay Chris wrote. It was dated 2/13/12 and was entitled "Your World." I would like to share some of it with you.

"My world was brought to life on January 9th, 1995, in a gigantic hospital in Little Rock, Arkansas. The first thing I did when I entered this world, or my parents tell me, was blow bubbles in the doctors face, I'm sure my parents were proud of me."

"As I was growing up, I began to notice one thing I really started to grow a passion for, and that was football. I remember being about five or six years of age sitting in my living room with my dad watching the NFL every Sunday, it was what I looked forward to each week."

"In my "perfect world", the only thing I see is my friends and family, they mean the world to me. My amazing parents have raised me in a way which I plan on doing with my own kids one day."

"The biggest help a guy like me could ask for would have to be having the best girlfriend any guy could ask for too. Anyone would agree with me when I say that having that one special person in your life only makes each day you live just a little bit more meaningful. Sometimes there is just something that's bugging you and you don't feel comfortable talking to anyone other

than your boyfriend/girlfriend, it's a real bonus that most people take advantage of. I'm glad to say I found one extremely special girl that I am proud to call mine, and I know she will always be there for me whenever I need to get something off my chest, having people like this is one good change that our world has taken on in the last couple of decades."

Words can't describe how wonderful I felt when I read this; he wasn't embarrassed to write about how he felt about me in a school essay. Now that's what I call extra special.

CHAPTER 11

Grieving

Before December 1, 2012, I had all of the typical complaints of a teenager. I had to get up too early for school (5:30 A.M.). I had too much homework. My parents nagged me to keep my room clean. As I look back now, I realize how insignificant all of those things were. I don't complain about any of those things any more. My heart is too full of grief and pain from losing Chris. He was the love of my life, and seeing him was the highlight of each day for me. He made me feel special.

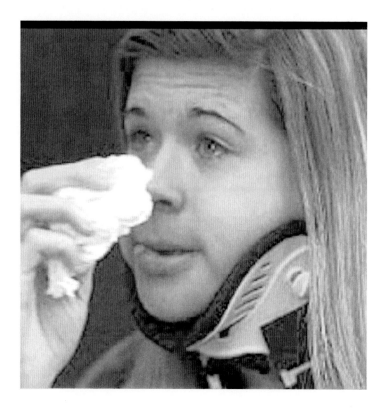

Chris and I were together one minute, and the next minute he was gone. I didn't get to say goodbye. I didn't get to hug him. I didn't get to say one last "I love you." We will never get to live out the many plans we had for our future.

I just woke up one day and was told that he was gone. After that, I kept asking my mom questions. "Do you think that Chris knows how much I love him?" "Are you sure?" "He loved me too, right mom?" All these worries flooded my mind. There was so much more I wanted to say to him, but I can't. I can't believe that I will never see him again. Never. I will never be able to hug him, kiss him, watch a movie with him, joke around with him, get a text from him, watch him play football, play in my pool with him... the list goes on and on. The life that I had with Chris is gone, and in its place is this unbearable pain. It feels like it is digging a hole in my insides. People marvel at how great I look, but flip me inside out, and I'm torn apart into a million pieces.

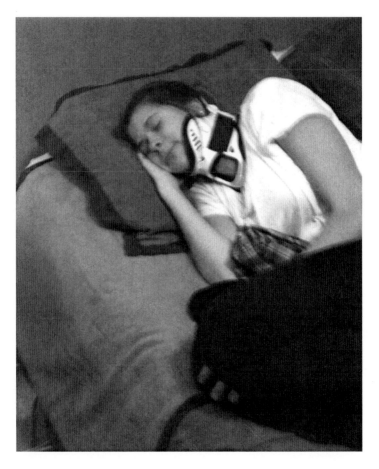

I found out Chris didn't survive the day of the vigil that took place at the Shen football field. The television in my room was turned on and there was a news report on talking about the upcoming vigil. There on the screen was a picture of Chris. I reached my arm and hand out toward the screen to try and touch his face. I wanted to be at that vigil for Chris, but I couldn't. Nikki spoke on my behalf and read a statement that I had written:

I just want to thank everyone for all your support and prayers. People should never drink and drive because it can hurt too many lives. Don't wait for someone to be hurt to be nice. Don't ever be mean to anyone. I love Chris with all my heart and don't know what I am going to do now. And I loved Deanna too. I'm glad that we were happy and had a fun night together that night. #69 is mine Forever!!

I have tried to keep Chris's memory alive in many ways. I recently got a tattoo in remembrance of Chris and Deanna. I am NOT a tattoo kind of person, and I have never wanted a tattoo. But somehow, it seemed like the right thing to do. My mom, dad, Aunt Donielle, and I traveled to Vermont to get tattoos in memory of Chris and Deanna. They are not "tattoo people" either! As soon as Nikki is old enough, she will get her tattoo.

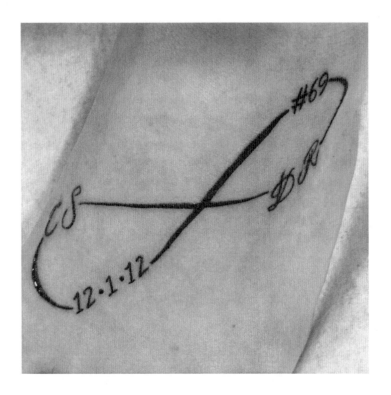

I am the proud owner of a customized license plate with an abbreviation of Chris's name and football number; he drives around with me wherever I go. I also give my friends St. Christopher necklaces and Alex and Ani St. Christopher bracelets on special occasions.

Everyone who loved Chris does different things to keep his memory alive. This helps with the grieving. On Chris's eighteenth birthday, there was a beautiful celebration at the Shenendehowa football stadium. My family was there along with all of the football players, coaches, and Chris's family. We released eighteen Chinese lanterns in Chris's honor and then celebrated at Buffalo Wild Wings in Clifton Park. Chris's #69 football jersey now hangs in the restaurant.

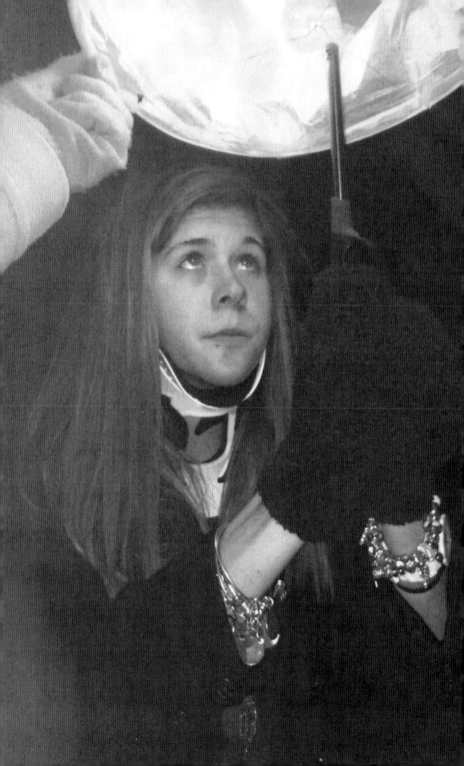

The Shen football team will be remembering him with a beautiful sign hanging above the door that leads out of the locker room. From now on, every football player will touch the sign before they go onto the field. It will be a new Shen football tradition.

All of these things are wonderful, but I will always grieve for everything that was stolen from Chris: his eighteenth birthday, our upcoming senior proms, our graduations, starting his life at college. These are going to be extremely difficult events without him. He should be here celebrating them with everyone who loved him.

My family had buttons made from Chris's senior picture where he is wearing his cap and gown. My friends and the Shen senior football players will wear them at our graduations. My parents had planned a big family trip after our graduations, and they were going to surprise me with an airplane ticket for Chris. We took our trip early, and without Chris, to help me in the healing process.

All I have left are our memories—our pictures, text messages, and tweets. I treasure them and like to share them on social media. I don't want anyone to ever forget Chris. Most people understand my motives, but some have not. One person continually accused me of exploiting my boyfriend's death so that I could get a lot of "likes." Why can't people just unfollow me if they don't like what I am posting? Why do they have to resort to making cruel comments? Do they really get pleasure from hurting another person?

To those who judge me, I say this: Everyone grieves in their own way. I grieve by reliving my memories of Chris because it makes me feel better. I don't think it is right to judge someone for the way they grieve. I also don't think it is right to tell them how they should grieve. Those who judge me harshly have not walked in my shoes. They do not know my pain. They did not experience the trauma. They did not lose their close friend and the love of their life. I struggle to stand in these shoes every day. I keep hoping that it will get easier. So far, it has not.

Please remember that a person who is grieving needs support. They don't need to be judged or ridiculed. They don't need to be told that it is time to move on. They just need to be loved and supported.

I will move forward but I will never totally move on. To me, moving on would mean that Chris and Deanna's lives didn't mean anything. I can't do that because their lives mean just as much to me as my own.

CHAPTER 12

Inspired and Bullied

The support my family and I have received since the accident has been amazing. We have been overwhelmed by the kindness of both friends and strangers. Handmade cards and posters were sent to me from schools throughout the area. My own school sent me notebooks filled with kind words from my classmates. Facebook messages poured into my page, and most of them were from people that I had never even met. Olympic swimming gold medalist Missy Franklin called me after "Missy Franklin call Bailey" went viral on Twitter. Miley Cyrus tweeted me, and even Greg Louganis, former Olympic diving gold medalist, called me.

In April of 2013, Greg Louganis invited me to be his guest at a taping of the celebrity diving show SPLASH! In order to attend the taping, my mom, Chris's mom, and my Aunt Doni, and I had to get ourselves to California.

The four of us purchased plane tickets and arrived in time to attend a practice session that took place on the day before the taping of the show. At the practice, I met several celebrities; they were all so welcoming and kind. Two NFL football players signed a football picture of Chris, and each celebrity took time to talk to us.

On the day of the show, we met Greg Louganis. What a truly special person he is. He wanted to know about my diving, and I was honest with him. I told him that I am afraid. Although my surgeon has told me that I can start easing my way back on to the diving board, I have fears I never had before December 1, 2012. My injuries from the accident were substantial and the recovery from them has been painful and difficult. I am afraid of getting hurt again. Can you blame me?

Mr. Louganis assured me that my fears are normal and understandable. He gave me some advice on how to handle and conquer those fears. I will forever be thankful to him for taking the time to give me the encouragement that I am badly in need of.

During all of this—the visits with the celebrities and the excitement of being in California—I wished that Chris was there with me. One of the competitors on the show knew exactly how I felt. He had lost his beautiful wife one year ago in a tragic skiing accident. When he heard about my story, he spoke with me privately. The words that he spoke to me were comforting, and I was touched by his kindness and compassion.

When I look back on everything that happened in California, I realize that none of these things could have happened without Chris. I know that he is watching out for me and helping me heal.

I know that Chris wouldn't want me to give up diving, and I still plan to dive for the University of Tennessee. It will take me a long time to get back to where I was prior to December 1, 2012. Right now, my goal is to improve as much as I can each time I step onto the board.

I will carry a lot of grief with me when I leave for Tennessee in the fall, and it will be difficult to be away from my family—my support system. But I want Chris to be proud of me. I want to live for both of us. I know that is what he would want me to do.

Chris would be so proud of the way that his family and members of the community have embraced me during this difficult time. Although I feel that I have been living in a terrible grief-filled nightmare, I have learned something important from this experience: the good people in the world outnumber the bad. I am reminded of this when I think about all of the events that have been held in honor of the four families affected by the accident. People put so much time, energy, and love into planning these events.

Although each and every event was wonderful and very meaningful, there is one that I was particularly touched by. It was the South High Marathon Dance held by South Glens Falls High School. In March 2013, they held their 36th Annual Dance Marathon to raise money for twenty-nine different individuals and eleven charities. I was honored to be chosen as one of these individuals. Prior to the date of the dance, I received countless messages from students from South Glens Falls High School. They told me that I was an inspiration to them, and now I would like to tell them that they have been an inspiration to me. The students involved in this annual dance put their hearts and souls into the event. They spend months planning, practicing, and finding sponsors. These students raise a lot of money each year. Last year they raised an incredible $395,000! It is obvious that the students and residents of South Glens Falls are kind and generous individuals. They really care about people in need—people who have suffered losses or who are affected by illnesses. All school districts could learn from the example set by South Glens Falls High School.

Many of the kids, teenagers, and adults that I have met since the accident have told me that I am an inspiration, role model, or hero. I don't see myself as any of these things. To all of those people, I would like to say the following. I'm just me, Bailey Wind. I am a seventeen-year-old girl who survived a terrible car accident, and I am inspired by YOU. You inspire me with your kindness and compassion

Through all of this, I have learned that the good in the world outweighs the bad. But the bad does exist, and I came face to face with it while attending a hockey game. Because Chris loved all things Shen, I have continued to attend Shen sporting events on his behalf. While attending a Shen hockey game, some students from the student section of the opposing team started taunting me for having no teeth. I had recently had a three-hour dental surgery and couldn't wear my temporary teeth (I call them my fake teeth!) I had two choices: I could stay home, or I could go out without my teeth. I chose the second option. Until my mouth had healed enough to wear my fake teeth, I had spent months out in public with a row of missing teeth.

At the hockey game that night, a group of boys from the other school kept yelling, "Bailey, where are your teeth. What happened to them? Are you going to sue for dental work?" The taunts seemed endless; the boys just would not stop. It was extremely upsetting.

After the game was over, the boys began bullying me on Twitter. Not only did they attack me, they attacked my mother as well—the woman who has done nothing but support and love me through this nightmare. They tweeted some disgusting things and even made up some lies. They didn't even have the decency to leave my name out of the tweets. No, they included the name Bailey Wind for the whole world to see. It was cruel and humiliating. I did not know these boys, and they did not know me. They knew that I had been in a terrible accident, and they got pleasure from making me suffer even more. Their tweets made it appear as if they were jealous of the attention I received because of the accident. One tweeted that I didn't know my fifteen minutes of fame was up. Fifteen minutes of fame? Is that how months of heart wrenching physical and emotional pain and trauma can be classified? Another boy said I had turned the attention I was receiving into a popularity stunt. As I write this, I continue to be speechless. I never realized such cruelty existed in the world.

Bailey Wind
@BaileyWind

No teeth!! Embrace it!!
pic.twitter.com/gelUNPLoIh

11:39pm - 22 Feb 13

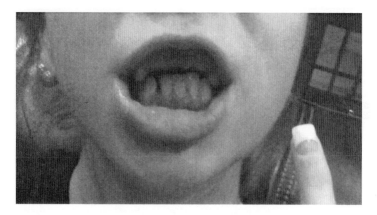

For anyone who thinks that I have enjoyed the
attention that has come from the accident, I want to
make it very clear that I haven't. Doctors told me that
I'm lucky to be alive, and I will carry this tragedy with
me for the rest of my life. It will also take close to two
years and multiple surgeries to repair the damage
caused to my mouth. Four specialists are working
on my mouth to repair the broken bones, gums, and
teeth. I am taking every day minute by minute, step by
step. I'm not looking for any sympathy, attention, or
anything from anyone. I'm just trying to get through

each day without Chris. I would give anything to
go back to the way things were before the accident.
Anything.

It is very hard for me to understand anyone that criticizes
or judges me for the way I grieve. While most of the
criticism has come from complete strangers, one of
Chris's friends told me to stop retweeting Chris's tweets
because they were hurting him. I responded, "It's helping
me." His response was, "It's hurting everyone else."
He also said many other hurtful things. Someone else
tweeted: "You don't realize that your tweets are doing way
more harm than good. It's like I take a step forward and
five back in my grieving process."

I can't help but wonder why people are asking me to
consider their feelings when they obviously aren't
considering mine. I know that a lot of people loved Chris,
and I know that they are grieving his loss. I am not trying
to compare our grief or say that theirs is not significant.
I just want people to understand that I am dealing with
a lot right now. There is no one else in this world (except
for Matt) that could possibly imagine what it was like
to be in the accident that night. It was a horrible and
frightening experience, and it will haunt me forever.

What do you think of my decision to use social media to
grieve for Chris? You may not agree with it, but I hope
that you respect it. Following someone on social media
is a choice. If you don't want to hear what a person has

to say, you don't have to follow them. Don't choose to follow them only so that you can be critical of what they are saying. And if you see someone who is having a hard time, reach out to them and support them. That is what Chris would have done for his friends.

I will continue to talk about Chris and post pictures of us, but I won't be doing it to get attention. I will do it for me and only me. You may not understand, but it makes me feel better. I will also do my best to be thankful and to focus on the positive. I will continue to appreciate all of the wonderful support that has been shown to me by thousands of people. But most of all, I will try to live my life in a way that will make Chris proud of me.

To all of those who have touched my life in a positive way during this difficult time, I say thank you. You inspire me.

And thank you for letting me share my love story with you. And most of all, thank you for helping me keep my #69, Christopher Stewart, alive.

bailswindy 5h

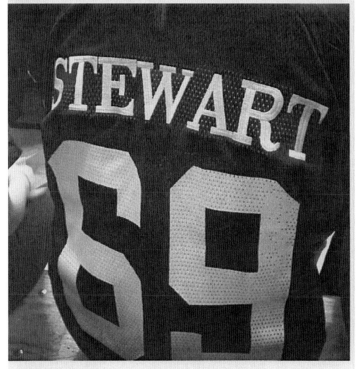

♥ **1696 likes**

bailswindy 69 is mine forever..I miss you so much..tonight was so emotional I did not expect to get this jersey I will cherish this forever..I'm your biggest fan Christopher..I love you so much #69

A Message to Christopher F. Stewart

I tell myself every day you are right next to me giving me the strength to get through every day. I still send you text messages every day, wishing for a reply. There's a huge hole in my heart and a member missing from my family. The pain of losing you hasn't lessened at all. It's indescribable, constant pain. I wish we were given more time together, but I treasure every minute we did spend together. Thank you for showing me such love and always being there for me. I've never met a more loving, kind hearted, thoughtful person. I feel so lucky that you picked me to be your girlfriend. I miss everything about you.

I will carry you with me in my heart everywhere I go until I make it to heaven. You will always be with me. I will live my life for the both of us and try to make you proud of me. I will ask myself in situations, "What would Christopher do?" instead of "What would Jesus do?" You are truly one of a kind, Christopher Stewart. I hope you know you made my life 1,000 times better. Shine bright like a diamond my special Angel.

No matter where I go, what I do or who I meet, one thing is for sure: #69 is mine forever!

Save me a spot in heaven #69! I love you now and forever!

mean it

Means a lot to m

Read 10:52

Bailey I'll always be here for you, through thick and thin, I'll always stand by you and your family's side and help however I can, you are all my second family if anything happened to any of you itd be like losing a family member. I'll always be here for you and you can count on that, I'll ALWAYS be here. Goodnight try to get some sleep tonight I love you more than life

bailswindy   ⏱ 4h

♥ **1004 likes**

bailswindy My whole house is decorated in so much stuff of Chris. I'm missing my boyfriend, my sister is missing her brother, and my parents are missing their son. Chris was a huge part of our family. Life is not the same for any of us and it will never be the same. We need you here. Its so awful not being able to see you or talk to you. I just wish

Miss and love you Christopher F. Stewart!